Madeline Sklar has brought togeth
extremely innovative way and has brought ~~ ~~~
knowledge.

As a feminist rabbi, I value this insight into the Goddess origins of our Hebrew alphabet.

This book is a most useful oracle in bringing forth one's own inner truths. It is beautifully and sensitively written, and rich with insights.

I highly recommend it to anyone interested in the commonalities between the Tarot and ancient Kabbalistic Hebrew thought.

Rabbi Sue Morningstar

In exploring the "almost fit" between the Tarot archetypes and the Hebrew letters, Madeleine Sklar re-introduces us to the *Aleph-Bet:* the 22 sacred Hebrew letters that serve as portals into a core understanding of Jewish mysticism. *Our Ancient Mother's Aleph-Bet* is not only a fascinating read, but is designed as a guide for practice. Sklar skillfully weaves the Tarot and the Hebrew letters in a way which is very much in line with Kabbalistic theory: allowing the ancient and timeless to come through by way of - and in relationship to - new forms and combinations. I recommend this book.

Rabbi Joshua Boettiger

Dear Madeleine,

Thank you so much for sharing your beautiful book with me. I so enjoyed getting a chance to spend some time with your words, with the depth and wisdom of what you offer. You are clearly a mystic, wise and talented. What an amazing contribution you have made to the worlds of Tarot, Kabbalah, and writings on the Great Mother, the Feminine.

This is a wonderful reference for those wishing to depend their knowledge of the Tarot. Sklar adds a feminine, warm, rich, and broad understanding of the way in which Jewish mysticism and the Feminine come through in the energies of the Tarot.

Rabbi Vanessa Grajwer Boettiger

OUR ANCIENT MOTHER'S ALPHABET
A NEW KABBALISTIC APPROACH
TO THE HEBREW ALEPH-BET AND
THE TAROT

OUR ANCIENT MOTHER'S ALPHABET
A NEW KABBALISTIC APPROACH TO THE
HEBREWALEPH-BET AND THE TAROT

Cover Illustration: Drawn from the old stories that describe the original letters composing the Holy Torah as having been black fire and white fire.

TABLE OF CONTENTS

IN GRATITUDE

Most of my adult life I've been filled with an ever-increasing awareness of all the things and beings for which I am grateful. When I try to enumerate all of them, my gratitude feels boundless.

From the depths of my heart I am grateful for Great Spirit, Great Mystery, Great Love, The Holy Infinite One, and for my life. I am grateful for all my amazing teachers, those whose profession is to teach and the multitudinous incidental teachers--more than I can count. I am grateful for those I love easily, and for those I have a hard time loving or even liking, and for the numerous people I barely knew and yet whose spirit and example opened, inspired and infused my life.

All were sources of some of my most profound lessons in the power of love, compassion and self-awareness, that otherwise I might not have had the opportunity to learn. Each memory releases a flood of faces and recollections. I am aware of the universe I carry within me and it seems limitless. And so I am grateful for all whom I love, for All that I love.

SPECIAL THANKS TO

I offer special thanks for the inspiration and support of Kent, my beloved husband, my children, my son-in-law, and my granddaughter who inspired me to write children's stories.

I also am thankful for, inspired and awed by the Members of my writing group: Ruth Wire, Cynthia Rogan, Joshua Hendrickson, Joe Suste, and Hilary Jacobson. Also, I am grateful for the keen eyes and line-editing skills of Sister-of-my-heart, my friend Keziah Daye.

I'm grateful for Rabbi Julia Vaughns' Jewish-linguistic knowledge, and for her astute sensitivity and ability to ask the relevant question to draw me out, and her editorial skills and support of my book, *Our Ancient Mother's Alphabet.*

PREFACE BY RABBI JULIA VAUGHNS

It is with true joy that I recommend the manuscript of the book *"Our Ancient Mother's Alphabet..."* I have had the honor of working with Madeleine over this last year as a consultant for her book, a process that has had spiritual integrity at every step.

Madeleine first gave me a copy of her book almost six years ago. I was immediately interested in the descriptions she had written about the Hebrew letters. As a rabbi, I am always on the lookout for credible resources about the Jewish tradition that are accessible and useful for people and I found her commentaries about the letters to be an especially potent and fresh lens that I hadn't seen before. Many people are beginning to re-incorporate the Divine Feminine into our understanding of the Hebrew letters, but Madeleine's work has a uniqueness that stands out from the pack in a way that resonates with me deeply.

This is actually the second oracle of Hebrew letters that I have helped edit and have consulted on several others, all of which are written by "amateurs" in a non-rabbinic, popular style, and all with merit—so there is something going on that is coming into the world to pay attention to. How can everyday normal people access the wisdom of the Hebrew letters and of Kabbalah directly, from the truth of their own hearts, without needing a rabbi or scholarly authority to guide them? This is so critical. And at the same time, to not have people playing with spiritual lineages in ways that are inappropriate and incorrect. This book and the oracle provided through it balance these points beautifully. The Hebrew letter commentaries are an exceptional example of an authentically received wisdom stream that has been vetted through a Kabbalistic lineage holder to ensure authenticity.

The correlations with the traditional Tarot and the way in which the cards as an oracle are presented, also are in keeping with the ways of Torah and of all authentic spiritual traditions, in the sense that the reader/user is encouraged to utilize the oracle as a vehicle for accessing their own truth and their own connection to the unifying G-d presence, and not as a fortune-telling device. Best of all, the oracle works! The deck and the commentaries have been tested in readings across many years and have proven their usefulness as a divine channel.

Please receive this manuscript with an open heart. Read the letter and card commentaries and test the oracle, either by making your own cards or by opening randomly to a page in the book. Your feedback is welcome! Bless you for your time in examining the merits of this book and this oracle.

In Peace, Rabbi Julia Melanie Vaughns

AUTHOR'S NOTE

When I finished my first version of *Our Ancient Mother's Alphabet: A New Kabbalistic Approach to the Hebrew Aleph-Bet and the Tarot,* I was forty-seven. After a two-year process, I counted it as my great good fortune to finally have it accepted for publication by Harper and Row.

Just as the final arrangements were being made for my book to be printed in China, two incidents occurred that sent my hopes crashing. First, uncertainty around the political situation caused by the 1989 Tiananmen Square demonstrations stalled the printing plans. Then, a publishing house merger, and creation of Harper Collins Publishers, resulted in both my editor and my book being let go. Feeling disheartened, I set the project aside, and went back to school to pursue my Master's Degree in Interdisciplinary Studies.

Twenty years later, I met Rabbi Julia Vaughns a legacy holder in the rabbinic tradition of the Hebrew language and linguistics. I gave her a copy of my book. After reading it, she asked if I'd change it in any way now that I've grown and evolved over the years. I brushed aside what I feared might entail a lot of work in the thankless service of a rewrite, and said, "No, I don't think I need to change it."

Then, I had an accident, while descending a steep staircase without a handrail. Two weeks later, battered, weak and immobilized by a neck brace, I was released from the hospital.

Home again, fragile as a glass animal, afraid to move, I felt lost and couldn't find myself. Then I remembered the last time I'd felt lost. After an ugly divorce at age twenty-eight, I'd drawn a Tarot card for focus each day, until I could move on and find my life again.

As I looked for guidance in how to go forward and recover my self, I turned, this time, to my own cards and opened my neglected book. When I reviewed my earlier work I realized how useful the contents were. I also realized that it needed a major rewrite. Bringing my increased skills, life experience and lessons to bear, I got back to work.

Now, two years later, I am thankful the original publication of *Our Ancient Mother's Alphabet* fell through. I am even grateful for my accident. And, for Rabbi Julia's question. All afforded me the opportunity, inspiration and patience to rewrite my book. When we can receive and express love for ourselves, and others, we join together with inspiring friends, where the learning and teaching are reciprocal and all are benefited.

As my evolved manuscript moves out into the world my hope is that people will find the depths of innate wisdom and guidance increases their own responsiveness, creativity and connection for the benefit of each other and the world.

ABOUT THE AUTHOR

Madeleine Sklar MS (Interdisciplinary Studies: Sociology, Anthropology, Psychology, with a focus on woman's issues)

I have been in love for over 46 years. My love and I have co-created a mostly happy family life, which includes our relationships with our extended family and friends.

As an expert at enjoying life, I am also an expert at being imperfect and accepting imperfections in myself, and others. Over the course of my 75+ years I have learned (and continue to discover) ways that can help bring more fun, more love, and more laughter into relationships.

I am a published poet, artist, teacher and storyteller with a lifetime of experience at continually working on increasing self-awareness that helps me keep growing and changing into a wiser, freer and more whole person.

INTRODUCTION

Hebrew letters are also numbers. Each character contains a wealth of symbolic meaning. For any given word, the numbers/letters can be added together and their sum, both as a numeric value and as a symbol, will reveal a deeper level of meaning for that word. The names and forms of the Hebrew letters such as ox, house, snake, and finger also carry powerful archetypal meanings relating to their ancient cultural origin.

The first known Tarot decks appeared in Southern Europe in the mid-fifteenth century and were enjoyed on the continent for card games. Although some claim the Tarot originated in India, Egypt or the Middle East, these theories remain unproven and the true origins and purpose of the cards remains a mystery.

Some believe it is plausible that since Hebrew letters are also numbers the original Tarot cards were developed as an ancient Semitic code and used by Jews, under the guise of gaming, for underground communications to protect themselves from being tortured, forced to convert, or murdered in Christian Europe during the Inquisition (which started in 1231 AD).

In the second half of the nineteenth century, French occultist Eliphas Levi (Catholic-born Alphonse Louis Constant) saw the deck as a metaphysical divinatory system. By linking the symbolism of the Tarot to the Hebrew alphabet, *Aleph-Bet,* and to the Kabbalah's Tree Of Life, he presented his Tarot deck as a potential map of mental and spiritual pathways.

However, Levi, with his Catholic patriarchal background, did not fully understand the Hebrew *Aleph-Bet.* He attributed the twenty-two Hebrew letters to the Arabic numerals zero through twenty-one, discarding the original numerical attributions of the Hebrew letters, and wedded them to the Major Arcana trumps of the Tarot deck. Levi also attributed the Tarot trumps to the twenty-two paths that lie between the ten

Divine attributes or emanations known as *Sefirot*.
These ten attributes through which The Infinite reveals Its-Self
are the *Sefirot* on Kabbalah's Tree of Life. In essence, Levi cut
and shaped the *Aleph-Bet* and Tree of Life to fit his own
design.

Regardless of any claims by Eliphas Levi and the
assumptions of other occultists, there is no conclusive evidence
that the Tarot was originally connected to the Hebrew *Aleph-
Bet* or to Kabbalah's Tree of Life in this or any other way. On
the contrary, the Tarot as Levi saw it doesn't fit directly into
either Hebrew system.

Nevertheless, the close correlation between the Tarot
archetypes and the meanings underlying Hebrew letters and the
Tree of Life intrigued me. It was a revelation when, in my
twenties, I discovered Gershom G. Scholem's then recently
published book, *On Kabbalah And Its Symbolism,* translated
by Ralph Manheim. Scholem wrote of Torah being one of the
feminine names of God. Since God and God's name are one, it
stood to reason that The Divine One was neither male nor
female but both and all encompassing. In expounding on what
Moses heard when he received the Ten Commandments,
Scholem recounted the teaching of eminent twelfth-century
philosopher, Rabbi Maimonides.

According to rabbinic tradition, all Moses actually heard
was the beginning of the sound of the silent letter *Aleph*. From
this Moses extrapolated what was needed at that time, for that
era. In a later time, our understanding of Torah and the
Commandments meaning could become completely altered.
Scholem further expounded on a belief, held by many
Kabbalists, that in a future era the letters will rearrange
themselves and even the meaning hidden in the spaces between
the letter shapes will then reveal a new, greater Truth.

As I read Scholem's work, imprisoning dogmas fell away. I
found in the letters of the *Aleph-Bet* the oceanic undercurrents
where creation happens and opened to the main vibrational
essence of this work. As they evolved, the sacred Hebrew

letters spun themselves throughout the cultures of the Middle East. Over millennia, meanings changed and shapes shifted, interweaving earlier matrifocal goddess-worshiping forms and cosmologies with newer patriarchal ones. Finally, their original intelligence became infused with the wisdom of their evolution and they emerged in their completed forms,
still containing their archetypal *Stream of Divine Feminine Wisdom.*

The Hebrew *Aleph-Bet* and language, underlie the Jewish mystical tradition, and is said to go back to the story of Genesis and the first writings of the Torah. This esoteric spiritual tradition and its interpretations have now come to be identified with Kabbalah, a Hebrew word that means "receiving." The origin of Kabbalah is unclear. However, it is thought to have originated thousands of years Before Common Era (BCE) during the time of Abraham and the origins of the Hebraic Mystery School.

Kabbalah expresses the hidden mystical dimension of the Torah and Hebrew Bible, which is the Hebrew name for the Holy Scriptures referred to by the Christian world as the Old Testament. Kabbalah expresses an attempt to understand the underlying essence of the Torah and answer the deepest questions concerning the human condition, the nature of the soul, and our relationship with our Divine Creator. The Tree of Life, which is the centerpiece of Kabbalah, forms a metaphysical outline of the journeys we take on our life's path, and like all metaphysical systems serves as a metaphor for All That Is.

When introduced to the Tarot in 1962, I was inspired to search deeper into the origin and esoteric meanings of the Hebrew letters. I asked myself if the shapes of these letters, and their potential to be viewed metaphorically could open a path to greater understanding of their true meaning. As I explored the relationship between the Hebrew *Aleph-Bet* and the matrifocal goddess-worshipping cultures of the Fertile Crescent where the Hebrew language originated, I felt as though I was being intuitively guided to new insights.

After many years of research, meditation and exploration of the Hebrew letters and numbers, I was moved to create a Tarot deck that better correlates the order and interpretation of the Hebrew letters to the archetypes of the Tarot, and thereby share my insights regarding our Ancient Mother's Alphabet.

I wish to make it clear that the main purpose of these cards is to be used for meditation and increased self-awareness. They are not magic fortune telling cards. No such thing exists anywhere, and no one can consistently and with total accuracy predict the future. All clairvoyant and psychic skills are fallible. To doubt this or to encourage another to believe otherwise carries with it much potential for harm. I have watched people give over their self-authority to healers or psychics or the idea of an oracle. It is never a good thing. Each of us must ultimately tune in and trust our inner guidance.

These cards are best used as a map: lines on paper that have only the sketchiest connection to reality, an arrow pointing to a direction in the directionless, leading us back to our Selves.

DISCOVERING A NEW CORRELATION

To correlate the meanings of the *Aleph-Bet* letter-numerals with the archetypes expressed in the Tarot, a realignment is necessary. The traditional pairing misses the mark, as becomes evident when we examine the first three cards of the Major Arcana, beginning with the Fool.

Most decks, that pair the Tarot trumps with Hebrew letters, join the Fool with the numeral zero and letter *Aleph*. However, *Aleph* is actually the Hebrew numeral 1, and metaphorically the *Aleph's* pictorial image-idea represents an ox (actually ox horns).

In *The Feminine, Spacious as the Sky,* by Miriam and Jose Arguelles, images of ox horns are described as primordially associated with the shape of the pelvic cradle and crescent moons. As such, the representations of horns were often viewed as images of fertility and the inspiring intelligence of Great Mother Goddess, through which all life emerges.

Also, *Aleph*, like most Hebrew words ending with an *h* sound, is a feminine word.

Further, *Aleph* א as the numeral 1 is said to contain all the letter-numerals of the Hebrew *Aleph-Bet*. Also, according to Jewish mystical tradition, *Aleph*, is naturally aligned with the oneness of God, The Infinite All. These associations clearly do not complement or enhance the Fool, whose meaning does not derive from oneness, from femininity, or from the symbol of the ox. Rather, the Fool is a masculine figure whose instability and fragility are the opposite of an ox, and whose innocence suggests new beginnings, and not the eternal and all-encompassing quality of the All One.

In Levi's Tarot (and the ones that followed his assignations), The Magician, the second card of the Major Arcana, is paired with the numeral 1 and linked to the letter

Bet, ב. However, *Bet* is actually the numeral 2, representing a house or womb, both deeply feminine symbols. Because today's Tarot stems from fourteenth century Europe, it naturally pictures a man as the Magician. This is in contradiction to the essential meaning of the feminine letter *Bet.*

The letter *Gimel*, ג, numeral 3, is designated to the High Priestess, although not one feminine word in Hebrew begins with the letter *Gimel*, while many stereotypically masculine words do.

In the pages that follow, I have referenced and arranged the traditional Tarot Major Arcana archetypes with Hebrew letters that share related essential elemental meanings. The discoveries that these new alignments open to an intuitive mind lead one on a journey of great beauty.

WHY THERE IS NO ZERO IN HEBREW

Hebrew is an alphabet and language in which even the letters reflect and express religious values, the most important of which is the concept of the unity and the all-encompassing singularity of God. This is why, unlike the Arabic and the European numeric systems, which later came to include the numeral 0 with its attending concept, *nothing*, Hebrew never included the numeral 0.

Philosophically and spiritually, the concept of zero, as *nothing* versus *thing*, is inherently dualistic. It allows one to imagine God is in one place and not in others, with one group of people and not with others, in heaven and not on earth. This idea precedes all other ideas of dualism--ideas that separate God from God's creation.

In Hebrew the concept of nothing, which we express with the numeral 0, has no ultimate reality. For "nothing" does not and can never exist outside the Greater Whole of the Eternal One.

All Hebrew letters are imagined as being contained within the *Aleph* א. The concept of nothingness underlying the zero is therefore viewed as being only a part of the One. Everything, all consciousness, all the seen and unseen worlds, exist and come into being through the continually forming, un-forming and transforming properties of the Infinite-Omniscient-Omnipresent One.

AN INTRODUCTION TO THE CARDS

"Every word of the Torah has six hundred thousand faces, that is layers of meaning or entrances; one for each of the children of Israel who stood at the foot of Mt. Sinai. Each face is turned toward only one of them; he alone can see it and decipher it. Each man has his own unique access to Revelation. Authority no longer resides in a single unmistakable 'meaning' of the divine communication, but in its infinite capacity for taking on new forms." (Scholem, *On Kabbalah and Its Symbolism*)

According to the legends of the Jews, it is said that the original Holy Torah was written by God in black fire and white fire. The black letters we see in the sacred Torah represent but a half Truth. To fully comprehend the meaning of the text, we must also be able to read the letters formed by the white spaces between.

The black and white give each other form. Each completes the other, and are therefore equally meaningful and must be equally read and understood. It is for this reason that I made this deck black and white, incorporating the forms and the evoked images of this symbolic and pictographic-ideographic alphabet, *Aleph-Bet*. The white and black fire of the letters dance with equal energy and importance, and in their dance reveal more of their true nature and harmony. Black and white together alludes to all possibilities of color. This unity of opposites encompasses all that lies between: Yin/Yang, female/male, light/darkness, positive/negative, thing/nothing, Being/Becoming.

THE CARD'S DESIGN

My card illustrations are based on or inspired by the visual simplicity of the original Hebrew letters. The abstract purity of the letter forms allows the meanings inherent in the individual letters to emerge, inspiring a more personal discovery of the profound truths to which the letters allude. The Hebrew *Aleph-Bet* has consonants, but no vowels. It does however, have phonics, which help clarify the pronunciation of words. In the later Biblical Masorete texts written around 200 CE, the *Dagesh,* or dot, was added to the consonants *Bet* בּ ב, *Tav,* ת ,תּ *Pe,* פ פּ ף *Kaf,* כ כּ ך *Dalet,* ד דּ *Vav,* ו וּ and *Gimel,* גּ. The *Dagesh* also appears with the letter שׁ שׁ *Shin.*

I wanted to base the deck on the essential meaning of the Hebrew letters. Although I am Jewish I'd never learned to speak or read Hebrew. My lack of indoctrination in the language, allowed me to be open to a unique approach. I read the Hebrew dictionary searching under each letter heading for the basic words or word roots that have been part of our human experience from the earliest civilizations.

The letter that begins each Hebrew word is significant in our understanding the meaning of that letter. Due to this, I found myself contemplating the common thread between many words that begin with the same first letter, and also the original symbol and number represented by each individual letter.

Meditating on the appearance of the letters, including the ones with and without the *Dagesh*, dot, added another perspective to my interpretations of each letter's meaning. I invited my intuition, my Inner Tutor, to inform or shape my interpretations. The process enabled me to perceive the letters in a multidimensional way. Interpreting the meaning of the letters, I experienced the way each letter was reflected in my life. With the evolution of my understanding of each individual letter, my interactions, observations, and life lessons all became interwoven. My interpretations of these letter-based cards are therefore not fixed, but are part of a fluid and constantly evolving process.

CREATING AND WORKING WITH YOUR OWN HEBREW LETTER CARDS AS A TOOL FOR MEDITATION AND SELF-AWARENESS

Although the forms of the letters as they appear in our Torah scrolls originate in the late second or first millennia BCE, their symbolic or ideographic meaning goes back many more millennia.

When discussing the Hebrew letters, Gershom Scholem in his book *On Kabbalah and Its Symbolism* describes the letters as each embodying a concentration of Divine energy. As such, each letter depicted in the written *Aleph-Bet* contains a wealth of meanings. These can never be fully translated into human language.

Because each Major Arcana card illustrates one Hebrew letter, each card's meaning is complete in itself. However, when two or three cards are placed next to each other, they may be read in combination as they may form word roots (a word root usually consists of three root letters which bear the concept represented by a word) or even words. Due to the Sacred origin of the letters, these word or idea/image roots are thought to be capable of revealing the infinite, multifaceted names of the Eternal.

My first Tarot deck was made with cut paper collage. Since it was hard to shuffle, I employed a looser, more casual drawing style using a black brush-pen, a marking pen with a brush tip, for the second deck. The two Tarot decks based on the shapes of the Hebrew letters are included as illustrations in the hope that they will provide an impetus and inspiration for you to create your own cards.

Your deck of Hebrew letter cards can be made using a blank Tarot deck, available in many card catalogs. Or you may find it more economical to use index cards. I encourage anyone to create their own deck. In this process, as you meditate on the letters and their numerical meanings, you can gain a deeper, more personal relationship with, and understanding of, the individual letters.

You may also discover, as I did, that the meanings and lessons of the Major Arcana. numeric letters, and the Minor Arcana, energies depicted by the *Sefirot* cards, resonate in your life in unexpected ways that can lead to greater self-awareness.

NUMERIC RELATIONSHIPS BETWEEN CARDS, LETTERS AND WORDS

According to the writings of the Kabbalists, Adam was originally created as both male and female contained in one being (Eve was one side, not one rib, of the unity). The word, דם *dam* (meaning blood) is spelled *Dalet, Mem. Dalet,* ד is the number 4 meaning "door" or "birth canal." The *Mem,* מ is the number 40 meaning "water." These two numbers (the 4 and 40) added together may be numerologically reduced to the numeral 8. The number 8 is the same number as the Divine Name, יהוה (the unpronounceable *Yod He Vav He* name of God) whose letters add up to 26, which also reduces numerologically to the number 8. The message hidden in this numerical relationship could be inferred as follows: That both the earth (*adama*) אדמה and Adam, אדם contain a reflection of the Divine Name, The Artist's signature circulating throughout creation.

Furthermore, the Hebrew language provides two words for creation, בראה (*barah*) meaning to create or form with an association with the beginning of a creation, and יצרה (*y'tzrah*) meaning to create or form by pouring or molding. These two words, numerologically, also equal the number 8.

The Torah, תורה is said to be one of the feminine names of God. It contains within its holy letters the sum of The Infinite One's creations and possibilities. Torah, תורה also equals, numerologically, the numeral 8. Finally, the meaning of the letter ח (*Chet*) which is the numeral 8, derives from an image that represents a field and the fence enclosing it. Thus, it can be said that this ח (number 8) represents the Infinite Self, as It-Self-Infinite One Being/Becoming, is infinitely selecting and pledging It-Self in responsibility to It-Self in all Its infinite creations and manifestations.

MORE ON THE NUMERIC VALUES OF LETTERS

There are a number of ways to work with the Numerology of Hebrew number/letters. One of the more popular methods works by first adding together the characters in a word to reach a sum. Once you've reached a sum, if your sum is over 10 add those digits together, until you end up with a number equaling one of the primary digits: numbers 1 through 9. If in this process your numbers add up to numerals above 9, continue adding the numbers of your final sum together counting by tens from *Yod*, 10, to *Tzaddi*, 90 and/or hundreds, from *Quf*, 100 through *Tov*, 400 that match all the numeral/letters of the Hebrew *Aleph-Bet*. For example the 4+40=44, since there is no letter/character 44, you must add 4+4. Your final sum is then 8 since 4+4=8 or the letter ח *Chet*. If once added, the resulting sum is over ten, it would have to be: 20, 30, 40,50, 60, 70, 80, 90, 100, 200, 300, 400 to be represented by a single character in the *Aleph-Bet*.

According to Abulifia, the leading thirteenth century representative of ecstatic Kabbalah, one should "Manipulate the letters and seek out other words having the same numerical value... And know that this will be your key to open the fifty gates of wisdom ... " (Gershom Scholem, *On Kabbalah and Its Symbolism*.) This study, which is called *Gematria*, involves numerical manipulations and comparisons between letters and words in order to uncover the hidden relationships that comprise the true nature of the Divine.

Much of Abulifia's writing was involved with the permutation of combinations of letters, and with seeking out words with the same numeric value or numerological values, which create a relationship between them. For example the word אהבה (*ahavah*) meaning "love," equals the number 13 which added together can reduce to the number 4. The Divine name יהוה equals 26 which, when reduced equals 8. We could interpret this numerical relationship as meaning that when two love, the Divine One is always present. Or, it can be viewed as evidence that the Divine One is a unity containing within it a love relationship of the Primal Two: the God Self that contains and encompasses all dualities, male/female, good/bad, light/dark, etc. Another example of *Gematria* analysis of a word is, תמה (*tameh*) meaning "impure/unclean" and the word תהור (*tahor*) meaning "pure/clean." You will find that by again adding the number/letters together and then reducing them to one of the digits 1 through 10, the word for impure equals the number 4, and pure becomes the number 5. Thus, there is always a larger potential for purity if we choose it. Furthermore, 4 plus 5 equals 9, the number of the letter ט (*Tet*) the image/symbol of the serpent whose temptation leads us to the knowledge of pure and impure. Since it is through the serpent that we are introduced to these concepts, it is only fitting that this is the first letter of both the word *impure* and the word *pure*.

TWO LAYOUTS FOR READING THE TAROT CARDS

I
FOR A QUICK EASY SPREAD

For an easy three-card spread, pull Past, Present and Future cards from your shuffled deck, and then interpret them in order.

A two-card spread can provide information, especially where weekly or even daily perspectives or insights are required. In that case, pulling two cards can offer the needed clarity, inspiration and guidance.

In both cases, as in the section on card interpretation, it's advantageous to center yourself and set your intention. Next focus on or visualize your question. Holding the cards, take a moment to breathe into your question until you feel you are in a receptive space.

An Example of a Two-Card Reading

After meditating for a few moments, I shuffled and then drew my first card from the deck. It was the *Shin* card. Next I drew the *Nun*. Significantly, the word "*Shin*" in spelled in Hebrew by combining the characters *Shin* and *Nun*. This double appearance of the letter *Shin* underlined the importance of the meaning of the *Shin* at this time in my life.

The *Shin*, the third Mother Letter (the first and second being *Aleph,* Air, and *Mem,* Water) is symbolic of a serpent's tooth. As the third Mother, Fire, *Shin* represents the destroyer of illusion, the fiery Serpent Mother. It speaks of a time when the solid appearance and apparent safety of our world explodes. Our life's meaning is transformed, awakening us to a new perceptual paradigm. For the *Shin* symbolizes the instantaneous and spontaneous movement of energy between worlds and even universes. *Shin* symbolically prepares us for the birth of a new form. She introduces a new reality, transporting us to the heart of All Truth.

Shin refers to a reality which occurs in a dimension beyond time and space, one where there is no need for energy to travel from here to there because there is no "there." The *Shin* represents that moment of equilibrium, which might last a second or a lifetime. We are balanced between wisdom and madness, as we are awakened and reborn into a new perceptual paradigm.

This really resonated with my life at that moment. After a ten-year experimental separation, I'd moved back in with my husband of forty-five years. My two fish and much-loved cat died. I learned my only brother, my baby brother, was dying and would be gone within the month. I was looking at the culmination of my two-year old personal injury lawsuit. And I was finishing the final edit of this book.

Nevertheless, I decided to gain further insight into this two-card reading, so I looked at the basic *Gematria* of the cards I'd drawn. *Shin*, 300, reduces to the number 3, *Nun*, 50, reduces to the number 5. Added together, 5+3=8 or *Chet*. The letter *Chet* is symbolic of a field or garden we have surrounded by a fence. As a garden we have enclosed, *Chet* is symbolic of our field of responsibility. *Chet's* connection to *Tet,* the serpent, who holds us responsible for that which we have chosen to call our own becomes obvious. I imagine Eden protected by the serpent. The three-letter word root *Nun-Chet-Shin* is the root of the word "snake," yet another conformation and echo of the *Shin*.

This was another reflection and acknowledgement that I was riding a major and inevitable *Shin* wave and there was nothing I could do but go with it. I was being moved by a force of transformation carrying me between dimensions to a new perceptual paradigm. This reading opened my eyes to the need for faith. Even if I don't know where the shore lies I have to go with the energy and trust that when I turn around I'll be There.

II
A DEEPER MORE COMPREHENSIVE SEVEN CARD READING

To use these cards for a deeper Tarot reading, I have found the seven-card layout shown below to be particularly useful. I was introduced to the Tarot and the seven-card layout in 1962. The woman who showed it to me said she'd learned to read the cards from her grandmother. Sadly, I don't remember her name.

I love the unique simplicity of her seven-card arrangement and have made it my own. I think of my layout as reflective of the six days of creation, plus the *Shabbat*. In a reading, this seventh card colors the meaning we give the other six. The *Shabbat*-card, as the last one drawn from the deck, is placed in the center across the questioner's Self-Card. Just as *Shabbat* is the lens through which we look back to evaluate the week that has passed, it also colors our view looking forward at the week to come. What or how we see influences not only what we get, but also how we feel about it.

Using your non-dominant hand, the deck is shuffled and then divided in thirds, restacked using your dominant hand, and shuffled again. This process is repeated four times. When finished, the face down stack is fanned out for the questioner to draw one card from the pack. This card, once drawn and turned over, whether upright or reversed, represents the questioner's self-at-this-moment. The rest of the deck is then gathered face down in a stack. Finally, six cards are drawn. They are placed in order of appearance, whether upright or reversed, in their designated position around the questioner's self-card.

See the following, "*Shabbat*, Or Seven-Card Layout."

THE *SHABBAT*, OR SEVEN-CARD LAYOUT
ORDER AND PLACEMEN OF CARDS AS DRAWN

1   The self or indicator card represents the person being read for in *this* moment, since as a living entity, who we are changes, even moment to moment.
2   The aspect of the past that is now influencing the present.
3   The immediate present. The energetic tide the questioner is being moved by.
4   The near future.
5   The farther future.
6   The outcome or end of the journey a reading is referencing.
7   The *Shabbat* card is first placed across the "Self" card, then over each of the other cards. It is the lens which colors reality. Like sunglasses it tints the way we view the past, present, near future, and even the outcome.

SHABAT SEVEN CARD LAYOUT
ILLUSTRATED

1. The self or indicator card represents the person being read for in *this* moment, since as a living entity, who we are changes, even moment to moment.
2. The aspect of the past that is now influencing the present.
3. The immediate present. The energetic tide the questioner is being moved by.
4. The near future.
5. The farther future.
6. The outcome or end of the journey a reading is referencing.
7. The *Shabbat* card is first placed across the "Self" card, then over each of the other cards. It is the lens, which colors reality. Like sunglasses it tints the way we view the past, present, near future, and even the outcome.

SHABAT SEVEN CARD LAYOUT ILLUSTRATED

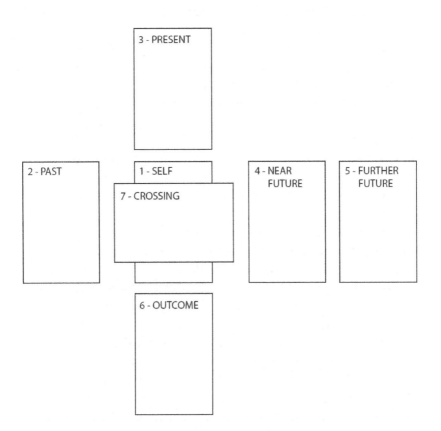

FOR FURTHER INTERPRETATION OF CARDS IN A READING

To gain greater insight concerning the meaning of an individual card in a reading, center yourself. Then, set your intention and draw from one to three cards to place over the card in question. I take a moment to follow my breath as I breathe into my question and allow myself to enter an internal receptive space, after which, I pull an additional card or cards from the deck, to place on top of, and, if needed, on each side of the card whose meaning I need to clarify.

If a card is reversed in a layout (as seen in the pages covering the meanings of individual cards) it may (as well as, or instead of the given negative meaning) indicate an internal rather than external or an unconscious rather than conscious process.

Another way to work with the cards is to look at the possible word roots created by the Major Arcana letter cards. Anywhere the letter cards show up in a reading, they can be viewed as an oracle within the oracle, especially if there is more than one letter card in a given reading. Extra cards can be drawn to clarify word roots. The remaining Letter cards, the Royal Persona cards and/or number cards from the four suits can all expand and further define the meaning that you're seeking.

As an example, when I asked if I should contact a particular individual concerning my writing, I pulled three cards. I got the letter *Kaf,* the letter *Shin*, and the Prince of Cups. Looking up words beginning with the letters *Kaf-Shin,* I found a number of words referring to magic or casting a spell, and also a number of words meaning "purity

"opportunity," and "to be ritually fit." Since the Prince card didn't refer to a letter, I first read its original meaning, "to be a message of an emotional nature." Desiring greater clarity, I drew one final card and got the *Nun* in reverse position. I understood this as a warning not procrastinate, waste energy, or lose focus on my goal. Finally, I added the 20 and the 300 together which then reduced to the primary number 5 *Heh* which relates to being in communication with Divine Spirit. In light of this reading I decided it was appropriate to call this person for a meeting.

A final note: it's important to take into account that *Resh* and *Quf* are so related that they can substitute for each other in a reading of a sacred text or oracle deck depending on context and surrounding letters as words are created.

AN ADVANCED EXAMPLE READING USING THE SHABAT 7 CARD LAYOUT

After looking up and reading the card descriptions in my manuscript, I extrapolated the meaning I could intuitively sense was most relevant to my reading at this time.

Querent, Indicator card: *Dalet* (4) Reversed

The *Dalet* reversed may speak of fear as being a stumbling block to growth.

I'm asked to explore: "What am I afraid of? What might be holding me back from an important, essential growth experience?"

Might this door cause me suffering? If so, what might it have to teach me? What do I need to learn?

In either case, my soul calls me to remember, that even in the depths of despair, I am not abandoned. "Though I walk through the valley of the shadow of death I shall fear no evil for Thou art with me..." (*Psalm 23:4*)

Crossing, *Shabbat* card: *Yod* (10.) With the crossing card both the Upright and Reversed meaning of this card are equally relevant.

In this position, as the crossing card on the center point, *Yod* indicates the simultaneous end of one cycle and beginning of the next. Following its ultimate contraction, *Yod* in its own time must expand outward again.

I need to withdraw into my center point of quietude, where the still, small voice can be heard.

This reversal serves as a reminder that, just as a woman in labor must combine work with openness, it is the same with all that we give birth to. Periods of activity must combine with periods of deep faith and relaxation for the birthing process to succeed. Some things must not be forced or hurried. That which we desire comes only when we, and it are ready.

Relevant Past: *Kaf* (20) Reversed

Kaf reversed may mean I am resisting a necessary change. It suggests that I need to soften my resistance, adapt, and go with the flow. I'm reminded I might think a change of fortune is bad luck when it might actually bring good fortune.

I must ask, "Am I holding too tightly to some thing, some idea, or someone?" I need to remember not to hold on too tightly, not to make my holding a prison. *Kaf* reversed reminds us that even Truth, if squeezed too tightly, too inflexibly, becomes a lie.

It reminds me, sometimes the only thing I can hold on to is the certainty of change. When I apply this to my immediate situation, I became aware of how long my husband and I had (due to inertia) imprisoned our selves in a situation that lasted at least five years longer than was actually needed.

Present: *Samekh* (60) Reversed

Samekh reversed may indicate the unwanted results of past actions or choices returning. I must ask myself if I'm rationalizing a behavior to attain a goal. It is a reminder that the end does not justify the means. This reversal warns that if I continue my present impatient course an unwanted transformative experience awaits. The time has come to turn around, break a bad habit, make a better choice, delay gratification, and/or sublimate or transform a desired outcome. All this is possible, for the nature of *Samekh* represents both the end of one cycle and the beginning of a new one.

Samekh reversed reflects the necessary difficulty of overcoming my bad habit of impatience. To move forward in a good way, I need to free myself from present circumstances in a careful, thoughtful way, while one cycle ends and a new one begins.

Immediate future: *Hod* (8) of Wheels Reversed

When the *Hod* is reversed, it represents industry carried to excess: overbuilding; overproduction, hoarding, and anxiety over resources and abilities. This can negatively affect my relationships and/or health. It is important to slow down, relax, and develop greater trust and better communication skills.

Here, I am again reminded to slow down and listen to other people's needs and interests, not only my own, so as to not burn out my associates or myself.

Future development: *Gevurah* (5) of Wands

My energy may seem to have suddenly drained away. I may question my original idea and wonder if my faith was misplaced.

I could experience a sense of loss or feel physically or emotionally drained. It is necessary now to protect myself and my helpers so that the mundane physical demands of our bodies and all that I ignored earlier are cared for. It's now time to heal and evolve, to come down to earth and become responsible.

All that is to be done is to wait out the bad time and persevere. If I do not lose track or focus and act as though the inspiration was there, energy will transform into even richer creative expression.

Once more I am reminded to slow down so as to not burn out my husband who feels overwhelmed by the labor involved of moving me back into our home, and somewhat fearful of the future.

Outcome: *Lamed* (30)

Related to the idea of lightening and all that lifts us up, *Lamed* illuminates the darkness, transforming and enlightening us. The white flame blade of lightning illuminates the darkness as *Lamed* throws everything suddenly into focus, into consciousness. Electrical energy comes rushing up from the earth. A summer thunderstorm refreshes nature and relieves a prolonged state of tension. Here, the sudden illumination brings laughter and understanding, which opens a new perspective. Thus, even with all our intensity and stress, my husband and I still laugh a lot together. For *Lamed* is the heart singing and the healing laughter which helps maintain balance in both the personal and even the universal realms.

Using Clarification Cards

Because *Lamed* was my Outcome card, I decided to ask for further clarification. I also wanted confirmation of my intuitive interpretation, and so I pulled two additional cards to place on either side of the *Lamed* card.

The *Ketar* (1) of Swords, the first Clarification card

In this reading, the *Ketar* of Swords acknowledged my choice to control my impatience, evaluate, and step back from my emotional investment in our process and progress, so as to gain a more objective view. It addressed the importance of retaining a sense of humor and cultivating self-awareness, even as I continue to concentrate and focus on my husband's goals and my own.

The letter *Aleph* (1) was the second Clarification card

In the chaotic moment before conception, before manifestation, *Aleph* calls on us to trust in Infinite Cause and the power of Love. The lesson here is that Trust is essential. The dance is change. Learn to trust that which comes from my innermost being, my inner truth and especially to trust in Love, the essence of all creation.

Looking at Word Roots and the Numerology of My Reading using the Major Arcana letters and Minor Arcana numbers

4+10+20+60+30=124=(1+2+4)7 expressing need for reflection, rest, renewal. My number cards 8+5=13; adding the 1 and 3 together I get 4 (*Dalet,* Door or Birth-canal, a passage into the world of matter; also meaning, to be birthed into a new life). Combining the numeric results of the letter and number cards, the 4+7 equaled 11, which added together becomes the 2 (*Bet,* House, Womb or Home). For further clarification of my *Lamed* (30) outcome card I drew two cards: *Ketar* of Swords (1) and *Aleph* (1) combined become the number 2 (*Bet*, House, Home, or Womb). Adding all the numbers together we return again to the number 4 (*Dalet*).

Exploring the word roots within this reading:
   In determining which roots would be most relevant to my situation, I look to see which ones intuitively jump out at me. Knowing the *Lamed* indicates Turning toward something, to be pregnant by someone, or something passing into another condition, I associate it immediately, with my move. Next, the *Lamed, Kaf,* and *Dalet* in combination become the root of a word meaning, "capture," or "being taken," which doesn't mean much to me here. However, *Kaf-Yod-Dalet* forms the root of a word meaning "destruction." I am destroying my present living situation in order to create a new one. The root *Yod-Samek-Dalet* is "to found (a building)," "to pile up or heap," "appoint or place a foundation stone;" it is also Strong or Mighty. Certainly, looking at piles of boxes reflects our hopeful creation of a strong foundation. Finally, when my outcome card *Lamed* is clarified it is joined by the *Aleph*, the root *Aleph Lamed*, "El" which refers to God the Essential Creative Energy whose help we will certainly need.
   All in all this reading was perfect in that it reflected my husband's and my challenges and lessons. I could see where stagnating forces had trapped our energy and restricted our ability to shift out of our present no longer viable living situations. The reading assured me that I was being led and aided by Divine Source in my struggle. It described and

clarified the process I was about to engage in as I broke the stalemate, moved out of the house I'd been living in for the last ten years and back into our mutual home and renewed life with my beloved husband.

DISCERNING THE TIME COVERED IN A READING

In a layout, the cards may refer to developments that might involve days, weeks, months, or even years depending on the querent's situation or question. Usually we can intuitively tell by the content of a reading how long that period of time will be. Intuition is my most frequently used tool when I want to determine the time period covered by a reading.

If more concrete information is requested, using the Minor Arcana (number and face) cards may be helpful, designating the suits as follows:

Since a year is often referred to as "the wheel of the year," the numbered Wheels cards can indicate years in a cycle.

Cups are associated with the element of water. As such they may be used to indicate months or lunar cycles.

Wands reflect the fire of inspiration and flow of creative energy expressed in The Creation. The six days of creation and the seventh day of rest could indicate we're dealing with weeks or creative cycles.

Swords because of their association with the element of air may indicate fast changes or days.

For questions involving the timing of events, pulling a reversed card may indicate unpredictable timing. Face cards may also indicate unpredictability with an emphasis on the querent's being subject to other people's control rather than their own.

MORE CONCERNING THE INTERPRETATION OF THE CARDS

You will see in the following pages there is a longer interpretation given for the upright meaning of individual letter cards. That's because in general a card appearing in a reversed position can be interpreted as having an opposite, or more intense meaning or internal process from that which it has when upright. Following the description of each upright card, the "REVERSED" heading offers additional possible interpretations that hopefully will help inspire your own process.

THE LETTERS

THE THREE MOTHER LETTERS

*Our earth is sustained and shaped by the three Mothers: א
Aleph, air (the 1st mother) מם Mem, water (the 2nd mother) and
ש Shin fire the (3rd mother).*

    The Hebrew *Aleph-Bet* has three letters, which are
referred to as the three mothers: *Aleph*, *Mem*, and *Shin*. These
represent, in turn, the three primary elements. The actions of
the primary three in combination, creates earth. The three
elements: fire, water, and air (the mediating element) also refer
to the three seasons: the summer, the spring/fall (transition
season) and the winter.

1 א *Aleph*, Mother Air is the merged Creator and creation, the
    light and the darkness, the Mother/Father, the dancing
    Goddess in her embryonic form, the Great Mystery, Source
    and Container of all.

40 מם *Mem*, Mother Water of creation and destruction gives
    birth to the world and all beings. It is She who sustains all
    creation, sacrificing anything that is not essential to the
    continuation and preservation of life.

300 ש ש *Shin*, Mother Fire is alchemical transformer, mother
    of death and rebirth.

1 א *ALEPH* OX HORNS 1ST
MOTHER-AIR

Essence: *Aleph*'s image as ox horns resemble the pelvic horns which represent The Great Mother, The One, which contains The Nothing and The All. We're called to trust Creative Potential and Wisdom, Inner Truth. Love--the essence of all creation.

Swiss Tarot **Magician**: Rider-Waite Tarot : **Fool**

1 א *ALEPH* OX 1ST MOTHER-AIR
DANCING CREATOR OF ALL

Aleph is number 1, the symbol of the ox, which in turn is a symbol of Goddess: *Aleph* is the number one and one thousand, the unity containing both the void and the multiplicity. It is the letter which, although silent, contains within it all of the other letters in their potential. *Aleph* is the first, last, and only One. It is The One that in its silence contains the nothing within The All. *Aleph* is the I Am, the primordial chaos, the moment of conception. It is Yin/Yang, Mother/Father, beginning, end, and Infinite Cause. In the dance of black fire and white fire *Aleph* is the macrocosm. *Aleph* is the undifferentiated everything before creation, the purest abstraction, the soundless sound before speech, the moment before the impulse to speak. *Aleph* contains the qualities of being female and male, old and young, wise and innocent.

Within It-Self, cradled in *Aleph*'s pelvic horns, the One dreams the Being/Becoming, the cosmic wisdom and infinite creative potential. This is a card of infinite potential expansiveness. Here is energy for chaos or creation. Before the choice of conception, before the cell is fertilized or divides, before it differentiates itself, before becoming, nothing or anything is possible.

Symbolic of the Eternal One, *Aleph* can go anywhere, become anything. In Answer to Moses (*Exodus* 3:1-17) The Eternal Holy One says, "I SHALL BE WHAT I WILL BE." Because all choices are open in the moment before creation, if we draw the *Aleph* in a reading, it is essential to consider what it is that we want to create. We do not walk on solid ground. We risk all. Knowing our selves to be created in the image of the divine union of opposites in the moment before beginning, all is in perfect equilibrium. Trust is essential, for the dance is change, changing, creating, destroying, and recreating. Trust that which comes from our innermost beings, the inner truth. Love is the essence of all creation.

The dancing chaos, unformed sound and primary energy of the *Aleph* card resembles the archetype of the Fool found in decks influenced by Rider-Waite Tarot. As Creator Magician the *Aleph* is reflected in the Swiss Tarot

REVERSED

If reversed, the *Aleph* card warns against trying to solidify or stop that which cannot be contained or measured. It reminds us to remain open and fluid.

With the *Aleph* reversed, we must remember that sometimes it's best to stop trying to make sense. When we confine our sense of what is Real, or The Truth, to a narrow concept, we only hinder our ability to unconditionally and spontaneously respond to the flow of life.

2 ב ב בּ *BET* HOUSE WOMB

Essence: Held and protected, *Bet* is "house" or "womb," our home before we emerge into the world. *Bet* may be empty, receptive, longing to be filled; or it may be full, as we begin to experience the creation and expansive movement and mystery of developing new life.

Rider-Waite Tarot: **High Priestess.**

2 ב ב *BET* HOUSE WOMB
GREAT GRAND MOTHER

Bet is the numeral 2, meaning "house" or "womb." It is that place wherein we are held and protected; our dwelling, before we emerge to face the world. *Bet* is the number two and the first double letter. *Bet* without the *Dagesh* (signifying dot) is the empty house, the home waiting for your return, a blessing waiting for the receptive spirit. *Bet* is first the womb empty, longing to be filled. Bet is the beginning of creation and so Holy One creates Duality as out of that longing *Bet* creates the first spark of existence; the first blessing. Thus, *Bet* is blessing and the beginning of structure or order, the beginning of creation. The world is created through *Bet*. It is inspiration and expansive movement. *Bet* is that which precedes our entrance. It is the womb that protects, nurtures and prepares us

In Bet, the undifferentiated I Am of Aleph forms itself into the Goddess; Her womb first empty, then full of life. Thus with Bet out of the One, duality is created.

for entrance into the world. *Bet* is new, virginal. *Bet* is the potential of chaos containing the seed of order. And so, with the *Dagesh, Bet* is a womb containing a child.

Because of its feminine implication, *Bet* is symbolically similar to the High Priestess in the Tarot, for *Bet* is the Virgin Goddess, who, out of longing for a mirror reflection, creates the Other. Within her womb forms the first duality, the first fruits: the first rain, the first-born girl, first-born boy. She is a Goddess of wisdom and fertility. In a reading, the *Bet* card refers to the longing for wisdom through and because of which we begin to create our selves. *Bet* also speaks of the internal growth necessary before the external can exist. Because *Bet* is also *Binah*, (3rd *Sefirot, Understanding*) it is a card of understanding and scholarship, of guidance and spiritual nourishment. *Bet* is the Spirit of the Womb of Creation, the loving home which sustains us when we go out and welcomes us in when we return.

REVERSED

If the *Bet* card is reversed, it's about being empty, as in vacant, uncultivated or unfulfilled. The reversal may indicate that we've neglected or wasted our blessings or potential. This card can indicate isolation, loneliness or emptiness that does not invite an entrance. It may refer to a house without love. *Bet* reversed may indicate our cup is so filled with longing there's no room for what we long for to enter. So have a good cry and self-pity fest. It's okay. Sometimes we need that. It's just there's no life, or potential for life in there. Then think.

We're reminded that this moment is everything. It is all we have. If I think what I have now is all I'll ever have, my only choice is to be happy or miserable. When we bless our moment, choose to be happy or satisfied, whatever our circumstances, our cup, no longer filled with longing, may then find true fulfillment.

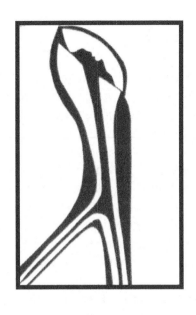 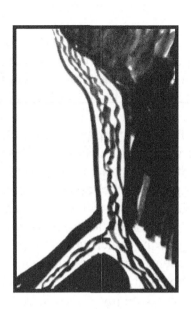

3 ג ג *GIMEL* CAMEL

Essence: Camel, Masculine Energy symbolic of any hollow object through which energy flows. It erects as energy flows in, then as energy moves through and out, it dies back, only to rise again in an ever-flowing cycle. We're not cause but conduit for Sacred-Energy.

    Rider-Waite Tarot: **Magician**

3 ג ג *GIMEL* CAMEL SON

Gimel is the number 3, from a symbol that means camel, for its ability to fill itself with and store water for future nourishment. It is the symbol of the throat, the hollow cylinder, and any deep, hollow object or enclosure.

It is the windpipe. It is the channel through which the energy moves, causing the tides to rise and fall. *Gimel* is male, mighty and heroic, rising up erect as the energy flows in, then dying, only to be resurrected once more. Like a wave rolling, he grows great and recedes, then grows and recedes again in an ever-flowing cycle. *Gimel* is drinking in that which is needed for growth, gathering in treasures and riches, gathering experience, reincarnating again and again, collecting lifetimes of experiences. In performing acts of loving kindness, giving and receiving joy, *Gimel* as gardener channels nourishment to our garden, and the garden ripens in return. Here we realize we are not the cause, but the conductor of, and conduit for, the Sacred-Energy received from *Bet*.

As Bet is the maternal womb of Aleph, the Infinite One, Gimel is the umbilical cord uniting and resolving duality as it connects and channels energy, nourishment and life into the newly created being.

Gimel, first child of The Mother, the Son card as primary-male energy, is about becoming great, gathering strength and experiential learning. It is directing, moving, appreciating and channeling Source Energy. The *Gimel* card also stresses the importance of learning the difference between what can be channeled, controlled or gathered, and what is beyond our ability to control.

The *Gimel* card is like the Magician in the Rider-Waite Tarot, for the wand the Magician holds reminds us that the power is not ours. Not being the Cause, we must release our controlling ego and open ourselves to become a clear channel for the Creative Energy.

REVERSED

The *Gimel* card reversed can indicate haughtiness, pride, boastfulness and exaggeration. When reversed, the card indicates danger of becoming hard and crystalline. It may also indicate we're feeling or becoming shallow, hollow, or gluttonous. There may be a danger of thinking our self to be source, instead of the channel. In reversed position we may be in danger of cutting our own throat by shutting ourselves off from our source of nourishment. When the natural flow of vital energy is blocked by our ego needs and the desire to appear powerful or always right, the *Gimel* reversed may indicate danger of becoming insatiable, toxic.

4 דּ *DALET* DOOR BIRTH-PASSAGE

Essence: *Dalet* is a door or birth-passage. Allowing our beginner-selves to be pressed and shaped, we trust and refuse to let fear block us from living fully. We bind ourselves to the One Holiness, know our true calling and fulfill our purpose.

Rider-Waite Tarot: **Empress**

4 ד ד *DALET* DOOR BIRTH-PASSAGE

Dalet is the number 4, from a symbol meaning "door;" it means both "womb" *and* "birth canal." *Dalet* is also the gift on the other side of the door.

> *Because the seed cannot rest forever nurtured in the womb of the Eternal One, Dalet is the door through which all must pass to be born into individual life.*

Dalet is the fear and pain of the one giving birth and of the one being born. So, although suffering, we often cling to the known rather than go through the door. We may be poor, risking destruction, or on the verge of dying and yet it is our door to wisdom, understanding and freedom. *Dalet* represents an opening to a new life, manifesting physically, spiritually or psychologically. Because even the most familiar doors hold the potential of something unexpected, good or ill on the other side, *Dalet* is not easy. It requires courage. *Dalet* is a dark unpredictable yearning and a green passage. All is lost, all wasted if we refuse to trust and allow fear to bind and hold us back from living fully as we travel our brief passage from birth to death.

When we move through the door into a new unknown, *Dalet* speaks of the required work, bravery, hope and trust we must have. It speaks of our willingness or resistance, to allow ourselves to be pressed and shaped. Because *Dalet* is the eternally in-drawing and out-pouring womb and birth canal, we find ourselves to be simultaneously the nurturer or the newborn sprout, the beginner, or all three. For it is the door that opens to our true calling.

Dalet is also the door our words open, the choice we make to speak or remain silent. It is the road into our center or away from it. It is the door through which we bind ourselves to the One Holiness until every moment is infused with trust; to know our connection as we realize and fulfill our purpose.

The card *Dalet* shares some qualities with the Rider-Waite Tarot Empress archetype since all are equal in the complete impartiality of her womb. She can represent indiscriminate production and the primordial capacity for nurturance and acceptance of all of creation. Like the Empress card it may be pointing to a time of blossoming into new beginnings, new understanding and awareness.

REVERSED

The *Dalet* reversed may speak of fear as being a stumbling block to growth.

An important question to explore is, "What am I afraid of? What might be holding me back from an essential growth experience?"

It may also be that we are too impatient with the time needed for the birth process. The seeming state of limbo, the insecurity of being neither in the womb, nor yet in the world, reminds us that this too *is* a place of being, this too is Holy ground. When we attempt to resist or hurry, the transition or transformation only becomes more difficult. Instead use this time to rest, to allow and to trust.

It might indicate the door to poverty or suffering. Even so, we may choose to view our misfortune as a challenge and invitation.

In either case our soul calls on us to remember that even in the depths of despair, we are not abandoned. "Though I walk through the valley of the shadow of death I shall fear no evil for Thou art with me...." (*Psalm 23:4*). We are not alone.

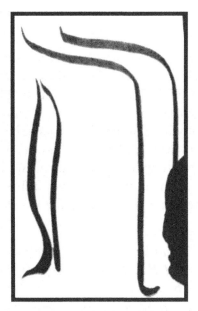

5 ה *HEH* WIND-DOOR
BREATH OF LIFE

Essence: *Heh* as Wind-door is symbolic of where we know ourselves to be inspired—literally, breathed into life by the Divine breath. We become individuated, begin to make our own choices and create our life, yet we remain in communication with the Mother.

Rider-Waite Tarot: **Emperor**

5 ה *HEH* WIND-DOOR BREATH OF LIFE

Heh, the number 5, represents a window or wind-door. Unlike *Dalet, Heh* is the door for air, for the breath of life. It is allows us to receive our first breath and return to Source, our last breath. *Heh* is to breathe, to be, to form, to become anything, to be changed and be capable of changing oneself. As air is in the space between beings, *Heh* is to be individuated. Yet as the air we breathe is the same air breathed by all that lives or has ever lived, it is also that which connects us to the Whole.

To understand Heh, it helps to see the evolution from Aleph to Heh as follows: Aleph is before beginning. It is the Great Mystery, all-potential, the fertile chaos. Bet is the beginning of order, focus. It is the impulse to create an other, a yearning to give life. Bet is the beginning of duality, the beginning to create and the first seed of creation. Gimel channels The Creative Energy, bringing this Source-energy in to nourish the first seeds—first creation. Dalet is the door through which all must pass to be born into individual life. And Heh is the first breath we take in order to become a living, individual existence. It is the moment we are inspired by the Divine breath, the moment the Divine enters us.

The number five, *Heh*, reflects our five senses, which awaken with the breath of the Eternal. Our fingers and toes, our four limbs plus our body, even the five seeds nestled at the heart of a cut apple all reflect and announce the sacred presence of *Heh*.

Now we are invited to spread our wings and fly. We can know that each breath is a gift and to trust the blessing of existence. As we fully experience breathing life as life breathes us, *Heh* is to answer, to *Shine* and to be fully present. We need breath to speak, and so in the sound of every word there is breath. So *Heh* is the sound of being fully alive, grounded, present. *Heh* is where we come close to the Divine Energy, opening the wind-door that breathes us and invites our participation. *Heh* is God asking us, as God asked Adam, "Where are You?" And we answering, "Here I am." Here, we enter the real world: Being, where we may become and express our lowest or highest. *Heh* is a dreamer, a visionary, inspired, and yet still practical, grounded and capable of turning our dreams and visions into tangible achievements.

The *Heh* shares some symbolism with the archetype of the Rider-Waite Tarot Emperor. The *Heh* has left the body of the mother, drawn a first breath and by so doing, has become an individual existence, a separate being, yet still in relationship to Mother. *Heh* is the counterpart of the *Dalet* the Divine Feminine. The *Heh* card may also represent one who is capable of uniting with the Divine in the act of mutual creation: Male and Female as the *Hieros Gamos*, uniting heaven and earth. "...he that looketh forth at the windows, showing himself through the lattice..." (*Solomon's Song*,2:9), *Heh* is the curtain that moves in the breeze as He shows Him Self at the window. The connection flows with love.

REVERSED

When reversed the breath is suffocated, all speech silenced. There is no air and so our vital connection is lost.

When *Heh* is out of relationship to the Feminine it is a mocker or fool, only concerned with worldly power. Reversed *Heh* is to be forgotten and to have to review the lessons that remind us that we are but a part and not the whole. It is rigidity and inability to be fully present for the other, an inability to love.

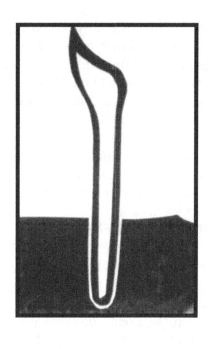
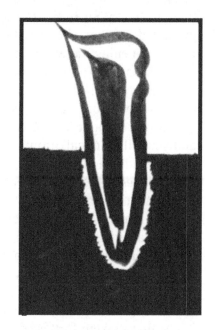

6 וו *VAV* PEG NAIL

Essence: *Vav* represents a nail or link to join separate
parts as we build. In building relationships *Vav* is to meet
and through sharing our depths, to be truly known. It is
the penis linking one body to another, and the child who
links us to the future.

  Rider-Waite Tarot: **High Priest / Pope**

6 וו *VAV* PEG NAIL

Vav, the number 6, derives from a symbol representing a peg, hook, nail, or link. When we need to build something, it is to assemble, to nail down, to put together. *Vav* is to meet, to share ourselves, to be known.

As a means of connection, *Vav* is the element with which we join the sometimes disparate elements of our lives. It is the way we link our lives with others. *Vav* is the penis, which links one body to another, and the child who connects us to the future.

While the Heh represents the individual still deeply immersed in relationship with Shekinah, the Feminine Presence, Vav is representative of the method by which this connection is accomplished. It describes that solid yet available Presence which links the otherwise opposite worlds of the Divine consorts.

We recognize now that we are each unique yet can work together, because *Vav* is also to engage in discussion and to compromise. Most important, when we confess, bringing to light the truth where there has been a lie, *Vav* is how, by so doing, we join ourselves to another. Through revealing our inner darkness and bringing it into the light of relationship, we allow ourselves to be fully known. It's about the need for self-acceptance and for accepting others for their unique selves. When we connect we become whole. So *Vav* can bring high and low together, linking heaven to earth, for to know our full selves is to know God.

The *Vav* card can be compared to the Rider-Waite Tarot High Priest, in that both archetypes address themselves to the ways in which we link ourselves to God.

REVERSED

If the *Vav* card is reversed, it speaks of the need to confess that which we might rather not reveal. It speaks of shame which keeps us from being fully present and connected to others and even life itself.

When reversed this card reminds us of our lack of compassion and conversely the necessity of developing greater compassion for others and especially ourselves.

In reversal the *Vav* may refer to a tendency to give away our power or shut off our ability for discernment so that others are able to shame us. By so doing, we may give away our authority, as we are wrongly led to believe that only they can create the connection, instead of trusting our own ability to do it ourselves.

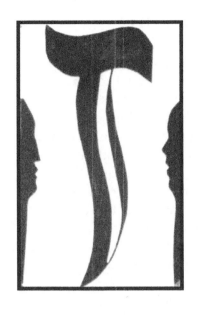 

7　ז　*ZAYIN*　SWORD　MALE
GENITALS
ALL THAT DIVIDES

Essence: *Zayin* represents a sword and all objects that divide.
It encompasses concepts of duality and choice. This sword that
divides becomes sword of desire, since the awareness of our
separation from original wholeness is exactly what compels us
to reflect, remember and urges us toward union just as *Zayin*,
the genitals, create the longing to mate,

Rider-Waite Tarot: **Lovers**

7 ז ZAYIN SWORD MALE GENITALS ALL THAT DIVIDES

Zayin is the number 7, a sword, a javelin, a weapon, and all objects that cut through the air, sword of desire. *Zayin* is the male genitals creating the desire to mate. *Zayin* is mating and the mate, wife and partner. The same energy that divides and discriminates, through the realization of being alone, separate, creates the urge to come together to be united with another. It is to pair and to be dependent. *Zayin* is movement: scattering seed, family, descendants to remember. When *Zayin*, the sword, is attached to free will, it can cut through and expose our greatest illusion: that of the "self-made person", of "I think therefore I am," the illusion we are more special than the rest of creation, separate from the Whole Holy, from God.

As the seventh day, *Shabbat*, it is the one day set aside, for us to rest and reflect on what has passed. We can now look back over the six preceding days and from that vantage point, that remembering, we are again invited to join ourselves to The Eternal and gain the perspective and wisdom we need for the upcoming week.

Zayin comes after Vav, for first we are linked to the Divine Source, as were the original Adam and Eve in Eden. Next, awakened, given Knowledge and thus the ability of choice, we separate ourselves from Holy Source, so that we may choose to be joined again. Our return, then, is on a very different level. Zayin is like the "terrible twos" when the child first realizes itself to be a separate being. It is this very thought which then creates the yearning for the perceived other.

It is a card of separation. Divided from our original infant-oneness, we begin to know ourselves and our parents as separate beings. Our dawning self-awareness divides us from Holy Source. We find ourselves expelled from our original Eden. The sword of our will bars our return to the innocent idyll of the past. We have eaten from the Tree of Knowledge of Good and Evil. Knowing choice, we begin to choose our own way. Now we may freely choose to remember and honor our dependence on the other, to realize that without the other we are incomplete, and to remember Wholeness, from whence we came. Since *Zayin* is also about discernment, this card may indicate we are being pulled in two equally tempting directions. It speaks of our need to make a clear choice.

Zayin can be an affirmation that even if we have doubts, we have made the right choice. When we remember and reconnect to Holy Source, we see with Real eyes that our intuition united us with a deeper wisdom, and helped us discern the right choice.

The *Zayin* card shares some of the qualities of the Rider-Waite Tarot Lovers card. The ability to separate ourselves from what we consider our not-self allows us to discern between equal energies and choose our right way. Also, our awareness of separation has created a lonely ache and feeling of incompleteness that now becomes the longing to unite with another. This ache, of course, is the very thing that brings about our joyous union.

REVERSED

When the *Zayin* card is reversed, we are trying to avoid making a choice. Where taking a long time to deliberate an important matter may usually be a good idea, there are also times when we don't have that luxury. Sometimes our very survival or happiness depends on fast, decisive action. The time has now come to cut through fearful negativity, trust our connection to the Divine purpose, and act.

This reversal may be an indication that we have hesitated too long because of indecisiveness or fear. A clear choice must be made.

The negative of the *Zayin* can indicate a wrong choice and our need to change course or make amends.

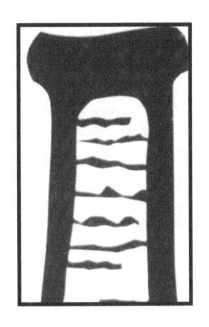

8 ח *CHET* A FIELD ENCLOSED

Essence: *Chet* represents a fenced field. That which we claim for ourselves becomes our responsibility. Whatever we are pledged to alters and transforms us. We love and are loved, creating and nurturing lasting relationships.

Rider-Waite Tarot: **Chariot**

8 ח *CHET* FIELD ENCLOSED
FIELD OF RESPONSIBILITY

Chet is the number 8, a field enclosed and the fence enclosing it. The choice offered by *Zayin* has been made. One plot of land has been selected from all that lay before us. When we built a fence around it we thereby claimed it for ourselves. *Chet* is to be responsible, to pledge ourselves. We are altered and transformed by how we respond to our responsibilities.

For our chosen land to be productive requires the labor of sowing and returning, then waiting patiently for our garden to bloom. When it does, *Chet* is to make happy, to bless, to love and be loved.

> *In Zayin our longing for union has led us to make a choice, and so Chet is the wedding canopy and the wedding, which also represents the choice to select one from among many others, and to pledge to our chosen one, our care, attention and responsibility. Additionally, the letter refers to friendship, to the commitment and cultivation of relationships so that they, like the field, may bear fruit in the physical, emotional and spiritual levels of our being.*

Wisdom begins with Chet. As with responsibility, wisdom grows when we allow ourselves to be penetrating and penetrable. When we recognize that growth comes through our exchange of love, energy and care, we share strength and vulnerability with our beloved. We are then able to continually discover the miraculous uniqueness of that other to whom we are pledged.

Life is *Chet*, as is freedom. When we are free we can choose that which we claim as our own. It then becomes our responsibility, even if to be free, to be truly alive, we must be willing to risk weeping a little, or even a lot. Thus, *Chet* also brings suffering, whether the happy suffering of birth pains or the agony of devastation, which is the inevitable end of even—especially!—the deepest love relationships.

The *Chet* card shares some meaning with the Tarot Chariot card for that which we conquer and claim as our own, becomes our responsibility.

REVERSED

When reversed, the *Chet* speaks of failure to take responsibility because we are fearful of vulnerability and/or unable or unwilling to value sufficiently that to which we were once committed. This may indicate a need for us to rcpair a pledge we have broken or relationship we have harmed.

We might ask, "Could what I want in any way result in the injury, conquest or enslavement of another?"

Conversely, it might be a warning that a promise made to us is in danger of being unfulfilled. It could indicate that someone with whom we are dealing is untrustworthy and trying to manipulate or enslave us.

We might ask, "Am I allowing myself to be coerced into committing to something against my better judgment?"

If we are avoiding or wavering in our commitment to an action, we may sin by missing the mark: in a half-way attempt to shoot an apple off our friend's head we may hit his eye instead. Through careless inattention and not being fully responsible we risk hurting ourselves or another. The ground we walk on is Holy. *Chet* reversed reminds us that when we allow ourselves to be fenced in by fear of suffering, we fence out life.

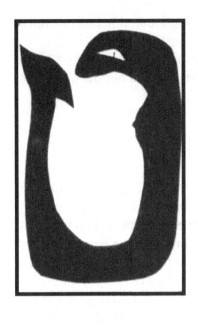
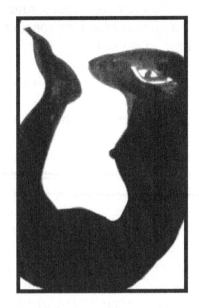

9   ט   *TET*   SERPENT

Essence: *Tet*, a serpent, symbolizes the Great Mother. The Wise Preserving Force and Lawmaker offers us knowledge and loss of innocence, then holds us responsible for our choices. Our karmic teacher invites us to know our Holiness.

    Rider-Waite Tarot: **Justice**

9 ט *TET*   SERPENT   KARMA

Tet is the number 9, Serpent, Karma the Great Mother forming a shelter or roof with her body. She holds us in her dark lap and teaches us her wisdom. She protects and covers us over and rocks us to sleep. At the navel, the center where the

While Chet is a fence around a field, Tet is the serpent protecting and surrounding the fence. Chet is a field or garden enclosed and Tet is the serpent of wisdom curled around the tree at its center. As the serpent in the garden who first inspired us with the knowledge of good and evil, she now holds us responsible for that which we have chosen to make our own. Tet is the truth we must face. Linked to wisdom and to prophetic dreams where the Divine reveals itself, She opens our mind to knowledge and our destiny. She is the lawmaker and counselor, the place deep in our center where we know whether our choices are right or wrong, healthy or destructive. When we are sheltered and immersed in goodness she is the hidden treasure, the wholeness that is in our own depths, a gift to be discovered. It is the miracle by which we live.

secrets of life are hidden, she is the shield and natural preserving force, the energy that breathes and lifts us as we breathe.

Now made pure, we are given the power and the intelligence to fly with the highest Self. The serpent that tempted us with the knowledge of good and evil forces us to grow up. We have what is needed for a safe journey: a foundation and the loss of innocence, for *Tet* is good. "I would lead thee, and bring thee into my mother's house who would instruct me..." (*Solomon's Song*, 8:2)

Tet is related to the Tarot card Justice. Here, at the center of the Garden, in the protection of her lap, we are taught and guided by the results of our choices. *Tet* is the natural consequences by which we learn; she is the collector of karmic debts, the severe but still-loving mother.

REVERSED

When *Tet* is reversed, it refers to those things we do that separate ourselves from our highest good or wholeness. There is too much concern with self-protection. We may be behaving in selfish and irresponsible, egocentric ways. We have grown too fond of the dark lap, sleeping curled and covered, even when She would have us wake up.

It is time to awaken and realize that it is only the hiding, the lack of trust in our relationships, the secrets we keep from ourselves and those we profess to love, that separate us from the Garden.

10 ' *YOD* **FINGER**

Essence: The image representing a finger or hand, symbolic of the microcosm, carries all potential for manifestation.
Withdrawing into our center we invite Holy Wisdom to infuse us. Complete in our self we can join others or remain single.
Rider-Waite Tarot: **Hermit**

10 ' *YOD* FINGER MICROCOSM A LONE FINGER

Yod is the number 10, a finger, or a hand. As the smallest letter, it holds all potential to become manifest.

Where the Aleph is One containing the multiplicity, the macrocosm, Yod represents the microcosm. This letter, like the recently discovered Higgs Particle, has a magnetic quality, which draws others in to join it to co-create a new essence.

Unique, singular and alone, although complete in itself, *Yod* still longs to be together with another. *Yod* is the gravity which unites, the yoni drawing the lover in, the moon pulling the tides, the Absolute Creative Essence, God in unison-- magnetic Wholeness. As the central point, *Yod* simultaneously ends one cycle and begins the next, for following its ultimate contraction, *Yod* must expand outward again.

Because the *Yod* represents the most microcosmic particle, it indicates the necessity of withdrawing into our center, our point of quietude, and it speaks of the place where the still, small voice can be heard.

If we are open in a state of creative rest, of expectant anticipation of union, of *Shabbat*, then inspiration will come. This is the time to wait and trust in the Holy One. We are required to pause, just as Moses at the Reed Sea did. With his hand (five fingers) and his rod (the tool or sixth finger) raised, he waited to be united with the seventh, the *Yod* of God the Divine Creative Essence. It is these seven together which cause the sea to open. The miracle can happen only when we are united with Creator of ALL, the Eternal One. Thus, *Yod* teaches us not to overwork or strain, but to combine work and rest, striving and relaxed openness. It urges us to become patient and expectant like the dry earth awaiting the first rain.

Just as the Rider-Waite Tarot Hermit card indicates an internal journey, the *Yod* expresses the need for being alone, having a restful and contemplative openness of mind.

REVERSED

If the *Yod* is reversed, it means we are trying too hard. We may not know or recognize what we have. Here, it is also the still small voice, begging us to stop and listen.

This reversal serves as a reminder that, just as a woman in labor must combine work with openness, periods of deep faith and relaxation for the birthing process to succeed, it is the same with all that we would bring to birth.

"I sleep, but my heart waketh: it is the voice of my beloved that knocketh, saying, 'Open to me my sister, my love, my dove, my undefiled; for my head is filled with dew, and my locks with the drops of the night." (*Solomon's Song*, 5:2)

Yod reversed reminds us some things must not be forced. That which we desire comes only when we, and it are ready. The land lies fertile, waiting for the first raindrops.

everywhere the dew
so small
the smallest inevitability

20 כ כ ך *KAF* HAND   PALM OF HAND

Essence: Symbolic of the palm of the hand in its three positions: empty to receive, containing another or grasping, and compressed into a fist. It may indicate a turning point. We are processing a change in outlook or outward circumstance, a change in fortune.

Rider-Waite Tarot: **Wheel of Fortune**

20 ך כ כ *KAF* HAND PALM OF HAND

Kaf is the number 20. Symbolically *Kaf* is the palm of the hand. The letter *Kaf* has three forms. First, without the *Dagesh*, or center dot, the hand is empty, inviting or letting go. The second form contains the *Dagesh* and could be seen as a hand gently holding another. In its third form, the hand is contracted into a fist, squeezing.

> *The cycle from the Aleph through the Yod represents the contracting of the energy to its center. As the central point, Yod simultaneously ends one cycle and begins the next. Following its ultimate contraction, Yod must inevitably expand outward again. Kaf with the Dagesh symbolizes the primal eternal microcosmic essence of Yod (as Source) surrounded by the many forms of the macrocosm, the eternity of Yod surrounded by the transitory nature of Kaf. The Kaf is therefore the Bet inside out. Where Bet was female, forming from her projected energy the beginning male within her, the Dagesh in the Kaf is the essential Female encircled by the Male energy.*

Without the dot, the palm of the hand is empty, expectant, cupped to receive riches and welcomes life's creative energies. The center *Dagesh* here is the archetypal and eternal, while encircling it is the specific and ephemeral form of the *Kaf*. *Kaf* is living life with energy and appreciation for the gift. It is the river of life filling and flowing eternally through us. We are always shaping and being shaped.

Comparable to the Rider-Waite Tarot: Wheel of Fortune card, *Kaf* is the sun that rises, shines, and sets only to rise once again, like ancient ritual re-enactments of the myths of a God-

King who, once chosen, crowned and exalted, is given the world and then sacrificed, only to rise again. In a reading it is indicative of a turning point, a time for changing direction, for moving on. It may indicate we are processing a change in outlook or change in fortune.

REVERSED

Kaf reversed may mean we are resisting a necessary change. It can indicate an unhappy turn of events due to the time or our own inability to adapt and go with the flow. We may sometimes think a change of fortune is bad luck when it might actually bring good fortune.

When this card is upside down it can be seen as an indication that we are holding too tightly to some thing, some idea or someone. Here is a warning not to make our holding a prison. *Kaf* reversed reminds us that even "Truth", if squeezed too tightly, becomes the lie. We are called to learn and understand the important distinction between holding and grasping. Sometimes the only thing we can hold on to is our awareness that life offers no security except for the certainty of change.

30 ל *LAMED* OX-GOAD UPRAISED ARM LIGHTENING

Essence: As an ox-goad or upraised arm, *Lamed* refers to all that raises and extends to impel an animal. It is related to the idea of lightening and all that lifts us up, eases and elevates us, and to lightning, which by illuminating the darkness, transforms and enlightens us.

Rider-Waite Tarot: **Strength**

30 ל *LAMED* OX-GOAD UPRAISED ARM LIGHTNING

The *Lamed* is the number 30, the symbol of an Ox goad or an arm upraised. It represents all that extends, uplifts or unfolds. *Lamed* is what impresses or impels the animal to some course or activity. Because it is upraised, it is related to ideas of elevation and inspiration. It is the serpent energy in the body, our animal self that can be raised through the center to merge with the Divine. By extension, *Lamed* also addresses the opportunity to be transformed or to transform others through learning or study. Aware as teacher we are also the student, we can be called upon to teach, charm or inspire, and by so doing raise up that which is down.

The Hebrew word meaning "night," *Lila*, is *Lamed*, also the name of the Angel of the Night. Within the body of the *Midrash* (stories or interpretations which elaborate on the deeper meanings of incidents in the Bible) it is *Lila* who educates the soul. She carries the soul throughout the universe, teaching it all it can learn in the months before its emergence into the world as a newborn.

The darkness of the night and the white flame blade of

Lamed had a special relationship to the Vav (6) because together they form magical number 36, the number representing Life eternal. Also, the Lamed Vav, or thirty-six truly righteous and good beings born in every generation. It is said that if even one of these humble, and thus hidden in plain sight, persons were missing, the world would come to an end,

lightning that illuminates and throws everything suddenly into focus, into consciousness are *Lamed*.

It exemplifies the strength the small must have to balance the great or powerful. On *Chanukah,* the darkest night of the year, it is the strength of a single candle flame that by its existence balances the vast darkness. *Lamed* is the summer rainstorm that refreshes nature and relieves a prolonged state of tension. Like the electrical energy that comes rushing up from the earth, *Lamed* is the heart singing and healing laughter. We delight in learning through joy, for that which the heart learns, the mind remembers. Finally, *Lamed* is the fool having the *chutzpah* to talk back to the Eternal One, and the miracle of the Eternal One listening.

The card *Lamed* shares some meaning with the Rider-Waite Tarot's Strength card.

This is a spiritual strength, a triumph of intelligence over brutality. It is not the strength that vanquishes or eradicates the opposition. Instead, it is the strength that integrates opposites and maintains balance in both the personal and universal realms. It is about gaining a new perspective. For like the lightning, *Lamed* is the sudden illumination that brings understanding and enlightenment.

REVERSED

When the message of *Lamed* is reversed, it means that we are too stale and weighty. Time to stop feeling helpless or pessimistic. Time to lift off our heavy stones of guilt. We need to forgive ourselves and others as we realize that the weight of blame, hurt, anger or resentment crushes our lives. The time for awakening, to become enlightened by a fresh perspective is now!

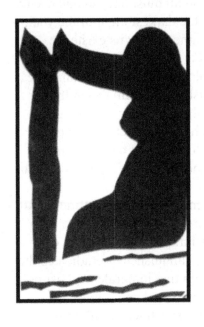 

40 מם *MEM* WATER 2ND
MOTHER-WATER

Essence: Symbolic of water, Mother of all life which shapes, nourishes, informs and forms the material world and all living beings. As water erodes stone, so must we dissolve our stony ego and false ideas of self. Our egoistic desires are sacrificed for the needs of the other. To grow we need to sacrifice our control, release the child and free our love. We must become open and fluid, able to go deep.

Rider-Waite Tarot: **The Hanged One / Sacrifice**

40 מם *MEM* WATER 2ND
MOTHER-WATER

Mem is the number 40. It is symbolic of water, Mother of All Life--the primeval ocean. The letter *Mem* has two forms. When used at the beginning or middle of words it is open. At end of a word it is closed. There are almost twice as many *Mem* words in the Hebrew dictionary than any other letter.

Mem is the number 40. It is symbolic of water, Mother of All Life--the primeval ocean. The letter Mem has two forms: when used at the beginning or middle of words it is open, and at end of a word it is closed. There are almost twice as many Mem words in the Hebrew dictionary than words of any other letter.

Nothing can live without water, so all that lives owes its existence to *Mem*. In the Bible Story of Creation, God is said to have divided water in two, becoming sky, or "*the waters above*," and lakes, rivers and oceans of the earth, "*the waters below*." Water circulates through all that lives, forming rain, sap, milk, and blood. It preserves, nourishes and forms our world. *Mem,* being 40, is also particularly significant because the number forty appears numerous times in the Torah. The most well known instances are the stories of Noah and of the Jews' escape from slavery in Egypt to freedom, where after forty days wandering they receive the Ten Commandments and become a people. Miriam the prophet, who insured her infant brother Moses survived by placing him in the river, and whose wells insured the survival of the Jews in the desert, begins and ends with *Mem*.

The Mother letter *Mem* is water (*mayim*). This Mother letter reflects the original esoteric meanings of *Mem* as representing the Great Water Goddess, mother of all that lives and the material world. She is Mother Nature who rules the waters within and waters without. She softens and shapes us: forms, nourishes, dissolves, and transforms us. One moment She infuses our dreams and knowing with Her wisdom; the next She is terrifying and destructive, mocking our helplessness and dependence. *Mem* overturns our reality and forces us to ask *why?* Both creator and destroyer, She circulates through our lives and reminds us there can be no growth without loss or sacrifice, no life without death.

She is the Eternal Question and Eternal Mystery, the miracle of life's inherent wisdom. *Mem* is also the water of the *Mikvah*, a bath where we are immersed and cleansed so that our old self may die and we can be reborn, renewed.

We now must become informed and, sacrificing our ego, plunge into unknown depths. Naked, relinquishing all nonessentials, we descend into the dark waters of our hidden selves so we might come up whole. Only then can we choose to become a *mensch* (a moral and enlightened person), an adult, an artist, a free person shaping our own lives wherever possible. Where we cannot control the circumstances of our lives, we can still shape our emotional response in the face of inevitability.

The *Mem* corresponds to the Hanged One in the Tarot, in that it doesn't represent a literal death or end, but rather symbolic death or sacrifice. The *Mem* can be interpreted as the emotional, spiritual and even physical sacrifice a mother makes as she releases her child to foster her child's growth to maturity, as well as her own.

REVERSED

When *Mem* is reversed the sacrifice is more painful or is faced with great reluctance. In either case, this reversal offers us an opportunity for growth and healing. Even when fate appears to be mocking it brings an opportunity. We can turn the hurtful stone in our gut into a pearl of wisdom and gather strength to share our painfully gained understanding. When reversed, this card is a reminder that, since *Mem* manifests in the material world, so the sacrifice and growth required of us must involve action in the world.

50 נֻן *NUN* FISH CHILD SOUL

Essence: As a fish, *Nun*, dependent on Mother Water, also symbolizes a child or fruit. More importantly, *Nun* is symbolic of the soul, which is viewed as swimming between worlds, integrating opposites as it unites the truth of what we are with all we can be. The Eternal sings in our depths.

Rider-Waite Tarot: **Temperance**

50 נּ *NUN* FISH   CHILD   SOUL

The *Nun* is the number 50. Its symbol is a fish. Because of its dependence on the Mother Sea, *Nun* also symbolizes the child and also any fruit or produced being. It represents all living beings that reflect and express the fecundity of The Mother.

Released from Mother Mem, the child Nun, no longer enclosed in the watery amniotic depths, begins the individuation process. While still connected the child no longer cries to its mother for salvation; no more does she depend on another to be complete.

The plunge into the deep, the sacrifice of the ego's need (required in Mem) has freed us, so that now we can see and finally accept, own, and own up to both our positive and negative characteristics. The soul has become an integrated being in itself.

Having risen with the Lamed and descended into the oceanic depths of the Mem, Nun is the child of two worlds. One face of the image rises up into the waters above (heavens) while the other descends into the waters below. Having been raised up by the Lamed and thrown into dissolution in Mem we incorporate the experience of each. Nun is the soul that dwells within our bodies and outside it in the Eternal realms. In its progress the soul swims between worlds and lifetimes. It is the truth of what we are and what we can become. Nun is the soul completing its work and preparing for its next development. It is the soul learning to surrender, to be true to itself.

Nun is that which is Holy in a person. It is the tiny spark of the Eternal singing in our depths. It is the music. Listen!

The *Nun* card shares some meaning with the Tarot card, Temperance, since it involves the mingling of opposites. Just as Temperance is preparing an interfusion, which at a later time will be ready for release, *Nun* joins the ocean of earth and ocean of heaven in its integrative dance.

REVERSED

When reversed, it is an indication that we are becoming divided by the temptations and distractions always clamoring for our attention. The *Nun* card in this position is a warning to not lose focus as we try to integrate the apparently opposite pulls of our life.

We are advised that while mingling our forces is important, there is some danger we may be succumbing to the temptation to dither away our time and energies. The *Nun* reversed may refer to a tendency for procrastination. Or, it may be an indication that we are allowing ourselves to become engaged with trivial or meaningless pursuits.

This is the time to consider the choices we would make if we were given only a short time to live. For the *Nun*, as our soul, reminds us that our days are numbered.

60 ס *SAMEKH* PROP SUPPORT
ARROW COMPLETION

Essence: *Samekh* is symbolic of a prop or support; also an arrow and all that reaches an end. It encompasses all concepts of circumferential limit or cyclical movements: the year, destiny, and fatality. *Samekh* references all that links ends to means, and beginnings to endings, so as to begin anew.

Rider-Waite Tarot: **Death**

60 ס *SAMEKH* PROP OR SUPPORT
ARROW COMPLETION
ALL THAT REACHES AN END

Samekh is the number 60. Symbolic of a prop or support and also an arrow, what these apparently divergent objects have in common is that they all lead to an end. The prop or support ends at the roof or other object it is supporting. Likewise, an arrow's journey through the air ends either when gravity halts its flight or when it meets an object. Just as a circle both encloses and terminates the flow of energy between inside and outside, *Samekh* describes all concepts, which pertain to a circumferential limit, circular or cyclical movements. It is therefore the year, destiny, to come to an end, fatality and the angel of death itself. Endings and beginnings and the journey are all One.

Yet, *Samekh* symbolizes a paradoxical ending. Because *Samekh* has a little tail, it can actually be seen to represent the beginning of an evolving spiral as viewed from above. It lacks the fixity of a closed circle (O). *Samekh* spins crossing over its original starting point as we spiral through our life's lessons. Thus, as one cycle ends another begins. *Samekh* is the cycle of destiny coming full circle only to begin once more.

In Samekh the connecting power of the Vav has come full circle, lowering itself down into the earth and then coming round back up to meet itself again in the heaven of its origin; from whence the cycle can repeat itself again and again.

Samekh reminds us that each step of any action or process is equally important, from a proper beginning to a satisfying finish. Beginning and end are one. What matters is to live with the consciousness that each day and every interaction presents a choice. The choices we make become us. *Samekh* describes how what we send out returns again to transform our lives. It refers to a turn of events, and also to turn around. It gives us the opportunity to transform ourselves. Consciously or unconsciously, willingly or not, we are transformed. We turn into death and return to our origin. We are transformed by lifetime after lifetime. *Samekh* is both death and infinity. It is the end, which links all that exists. Even death ends in the Eternal Infinite Holy One.

In its power for transformation the *Samekh* card resembles the Tarot's Death Card.

REVERSED

When reversed in a reading, this card may be indicative of the results of past actions returning or of our past catching up with us.

The contrary *Samekh* card is also an indication that we are rationalizing our means in order to attain a goal. We are being reminded that the end does not justify the means. This reversal warns that we are heading for a difficult time ahead. If we do not turn from our present course of action an unwanted transformative experience awaits us. The time has come to ask our self, "What do I need to turn around or return to? Is there a bad habit I need to break? Can I make a better choice or come up with a more effective solution?"

This may be a time to delay gratification, sublimate or transform our desires. And this is possible, for *Samekh* represents both the end of a cycle and the beginning of a new one.

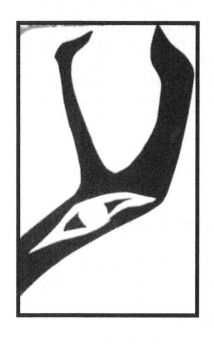
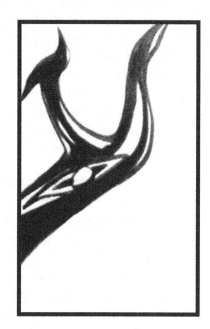

70 ע *AYIN* EYE

Essence: Symbolically an eye, *Ayin* is the beholder, the way we see and how that what we see, influences us. We need to see clearly to differentiate between truth and fiction to avoid being trapped in illusion. *How* we see is what we get.

Rider-Waite Tarot: **The Devil**

70 ע *AYIN* EYE EYE OF THE BEHOLDER

The *Ayin* is the number 70. Symbolically, the *Ayin* is an eye. It is with our eyes that we are able to perceive and differentiate old from new, age from youth, day from night. It is the discerning eye, capable of discriminating between appearances. Yet, like a two-edged sword, the eye can also fool and entrap us through appearances.

> *Just as Samekh, 60, is in relationship with Vav, 6, Ayin, 70, is intimately connected to the Zayin, 7, the sword that divides. In Samekh the end of a cycle has been reached and simultaneously a new one begins. In following Samekh, Ayin is that which contains the seed of the new cycle. As it rests within the dark earth depths of the sacred eye of Ayin, we are given the opportunity to see with greater consciousness, and so to create our world anew.*

Provided the clarity to see the past, we are now capable of reviewing our present. We can therefore choose our future with greater freedom. *Ayin* has tremendous power. The shape of our future is created by our skill to visualize or imagine not only a desired outcome, but also by our capacity to picture the steps needed for its completion. The better we can imagine and envision an outcome with our mind's eye, the more creative power we have to manifest it.

Finally, with *Ayin* we can open our eyes and awaken to the reality that we are not alone. In the receptive simplicity of a quiet heart lies the source of the most profound joy. No matter the outer circumstances, if we choose, we can see and realize Life as Paradise—this world, this time, *is* The Garden.

Ayin is the eye that can perceive Truth or, being fooled, can enslave, or entrap us in a purely materialist vision of reality. The *Ayin* when reversed is in some ways comparable to the Devil in the Rider-Waite Tarot.

REVERSED

The contrary position of the *Ayin* card suggests we examine the possibility that we are being fooled or enslaved by appearances. We need to remember the hand is often faster than the eye.

We may be lamenting the advantage our neighbor appears to have while ignoring or failing to see our own gifts. If we compare ourselves to others whom we believe have more than we ourselves do—or, worse, whom we believe to *be* more than we are—it is our eyes' distorted view that has ensnared us.

The *Ayin* reversed is the eye of the beholder who has lost sight of the truth that it is not our absolute or objective differences that feed envy, but our subjective perceptions. Blinded by a clouded lens of ignorance, we become enslaved by appearances and entangled in a forest of twisted branches. Deceived, we torture and enslave ourselves and others with hate and xenophobia. Entrapped by false visions, we are in turn tortured and twisted by anger, greed, envy, competitiveness, and ruthless ambition.

At any time we always have the choice to recognize that all this agony is our own self-deception. The moment we see that it is our point of view that enslaves us, we become free. The reversed *Ayin* directs us to look at the ways we have enslaved ourselves and remember that often that which seems real is only so from a point of view.

Ayin is an eye silently watching, waiting for us to open our eyes and realize that *how* we see is what we get.

At any time we always have the choice to recognize that all this agony is our own self-deception. The moment we see that it is our point of view that enslaves us, we become free. The reversed *Ayin* directs us to look at the ways we have enslaved ourselves and remember that often that which seems so real is only a point of view.

Ayin is an eye silently watching, waiting for us to open our eyes and realize that how we see is what we get.

80   כפ   *PE* MOUTH   FRONT OF THE FACE

Essence: *Pe* symbolizes the front of the face, especially the mouth. It expresses a point of view or judgment; it teaches or offers a blessing. Our words can build rigid towers of ideas, curse, inform, share wisdom or offer healing. The mouth *Pe* reminds us that whatever we feed on, literally or symbolically, becomes us.

Rider-Waite Tarot: **Tower**

80 פ ף *PE* MOUTH FRONT OF THE FACE

Pe is the number 80. It is symbolic of the front of the face and specifically the mouth. *Pe* has two forms. The first appears at the beginning and middle of a word. The second form is at the end.

While Ayin, 70, is the eye that forms our point of view, Pe, 80, is the mouth: what we tell ourselves, and the words we speak. It is how we express our perception of reality, our truth and values. In Chet, the number 8, we have chosen our field of responsibility. We have given our pledge. Pe, the number 80, is the mouth that makes that pledge, that vow.

Pe speaks of our ability to learn by word-of-mouth and our awareness of what we choose to nourish in ourselves, and others. By so doing we effect not only our values and judgments, but can influence others, as well. *Pe* is the use to which our mouth is put: to debate, argue, philosophize, judge, clarify and explain. With our mouth we can express with eloquence the benediction of the heart or, overwhelmed with awe, remain speechless before beauty. Thus, the mouth is the beginning and end of words, that which we can describe or define and that which is beyond our power of speech. *Pe* reminds us that clear communication is important to any relationship, and to be mindful of what is taken in by or goes out from our mouth. If we nourish and express our sense of connection to the whole and offer gratitude for our place, we open ourselves to goodness. If we are greedy, unsatisfied and complaining, nothing good can come, for even if it did, we'd never recognize it. We are called upon to strive to tell ourselves the truth, and to be aware of how, and if, we choose to communicate it.

The *Pe* card shares some meanings with the Rider-Waite Tarot card the Tower. For it is the words we use that give form to our ideas and beliefs. Thoughts formed by the words we use to describe our feelings and experiences, create the towers of our reality. These structures are useful when they help us understand our world and protect us from chaos. Nevertheless, we must always remain flexible, leaving room to attend to voices other than our own, so our reality can expand to be nourished by new ideas and experiences.

REVERSED

Pe reversed is more like the traditional Tower card. Our towering ideas and ideals, rigidly held, have imprisoned us in a tower built from pride, fear and egocentricity. We are locked in our own tower of babble until the lightning of life knocks it down. When our supposedly invulnerable towers are shattered by some unanticipated cataclysmic event, we are forced to an awareness of our vulnerability. It produces the change necessary for our deliverance.

In reversal, *Pe* may be informing us that we have been afraid to take individual responsibility; we have feared the risk of speaking out for ourselves. We have not spoken out against injustice, which offends our ethics and morality.

We are being warned to resist the temptation to exaggerate or lie, to be a troublemaker, to babble and to destroy. The *Pe* upside down reminds us to watch our words, be conscious of the possible ramifications of what we say. Even if we do not intend harm, taken the wrong way our words can cause havoc. Words that pass vicious judgments on others or that spread gossip create division or destruction. It can be a warning that we are the subject of such gossip. We need to be wary of those words which spread falsehoods and create philosophies that can lead us to destruction. We need to be careful that we understand what is truly meant. Also, we need to be mindful that by our words we are not creating misunderstandings.

We are being warned to resist the temptation to exaggerate or lie, to be a troublemaker, to babble and to destroy. The *Pe* upside down reminds us to watch our words be conscious of the possible ramifications of what we say. Even if we do not intend harm, our words taken the wrong way can cause havoc. Words passing vicious judgments on others and spreading gossip, create division or destruction. It can be a warning that we are the subject of such gossip. We need to be wary of other's words, which spread falsehoods and create philosophies that can lead us to destruction. We need to be careful that we understand what is truly meant. Also we need to be mindful that by our words we are not creating misunderstandings.

Only if *Pe* is reversed may the lesson, growth and illumination come in the form of physical or spiritual cataclysm. The shattering of illusions, the false or no longer useful tower we have built, however painful, can bring new opportunities and nourishment for our renewal. We may find that the shattering of our tower can be a liberating experience. It may actually be a great gift. From the destruction of our tower we learn that we live most fully when we know ourselves to be part of a greater whole.

90   צ   *TZADDI*   FISH-HOOK

Essence: *Tzaddi* is symbolic of a fishhook. Now we can draw up nourishment from the depths and gather gifts, both for ourselves and to share with others. Righteousness and goodness connect us to each other and Divine Source. We can fulfill our purpose to share our authentic selves.

Rider-Waite Tarot: **The Star**

90 צ *TZADDI* FISH-HOOK

Tzaddi is the number 90. It is symbolic of a fishhook. *Tzaddi* is the means by which we dip down into the dark Waters. In the depths of our own unconscious, we find, glistening in the murky deep, that our connection to the Mother's Wisdom waits. Our responsibility is to know that the gifts we now draw up are not only for our own use and edification, not only for our individual development. They must be shared. *Tzaddi,* righteousness, is a reminder that a gift is nothing unless it is shared. It was through and for sharing that the earth was created.

While Pe, 80, is the mouth, Tzaddi, 90, is the fishhook with which we lure and catch what we choose to nourish ourselves with. As the number 90, Tzaddi is a faceted reflection of Tet, 9, the Wise Serpent who led us to the knowledge of good and evil, and now demands that it be used and shared for the good of all.

When we can only fish with our hands, we are lucky to catch enough fish to feed ourselves. But with a fishhook enough may be caught to feed a family, providing sustenance both for ourselves, others and for the world. Sharing is so important; it is said that without the selfless acts of giving by the thirty-six *Tzadiks,* or righteous ones, the earth itself would perish. The use we make of our acquired wisdom and experience reflects our choice to nourish others or only our greed. *Tzaddi* is to serve and sustain others in the multi-hued joy of creation as we give back to the world the products of our rich accumulation. Eternally capable of giving and receiving, we can draw down inspiration from the Divine Source to put to practical use. We find food for body and soul, for ourselves and for the community at large. We realize our most profound and important purpose in this life is to share ourselves. *Tzaddi* symbolizes the goal or end toward which all Good tends, and the means to attain it as well.

Tzaddi shares symbolism with the Rider-Waite Tarot card, The Star, as it simultaneously reaches up into the heavens for inspiration, and plunges down into the depths, in order to obtain and share the fruits of Divine revelation.

REVERSED

When reversed *Tzaddi* is a warning against hoarding. We need to ask ourselves, "Am I being miserly?"

"What and how much do I need to feel secure?"

"What is holding me back from sharing?"

"What am I afraid of losing?"

If we feed our emotional projections such as fear, envy, jealousy and prejudice, these projections interfere with our ability to give of our self. It may also be that we undervalue our own gifts because we are comparing them to others and need to recognize our uniqueness. We need to remind ourselves that nevertheless this is what we are here for. If we don't hold back, but instead give of our authentic selves with a full heart, it is enough.

It may also be reversed because we lack inspiration. In that case we might ask ourselves, "What can I do to feel creative and inspired?"

"What action will help me stimulate and awaken my inspiration?"

The *Tzaddi* card is upside down because we need to be reminded that in the bounty of the Divine giving and receiving, there is no lack and therefore no necessity for fear.

100 ק *QUF* **BACK OF THE HEAD**
APE   MOON

Essence: Signifying the back of the head, an ape or monkey,
Quf begins our return to Wholeness. If we cry out to the Holy
One from our dark brokenness, The Holy One then cries out for
us. When we face our shadow we can know and heal our
darkness and become whole.

  Rider-Waite Tarot: **The Moon**

100 ק *QUF*   BACK OF THE HEAD   APE
OR MONKEY   MOON

Quf is the number one hundred. It signifies the back of the head and may also signify a monkey or ape or our primitive undeveloped self. Just as the moon can only reflect the sun but not initiate its own light. As the number one hundred, *Quf* maintains multiple relationships with both the Infinite one *Aleph*, and the ifinitely small *Yod*, ten. It is also symbolic of the moon since the visible moon is always in transition from undeveloped to fullness and back again.

Where the number Aleph, 1, is symbolic of the beginning of expansion into the multiplicity of the macrocosm, and the Yod, 10, expresses an inward, microcosmic journey, Quf, 100, is the beginning of the journey back to the whole holiness of the One. By embracing and integrating our shadow, we begin our journey to wholeness.

Ayin, 70, our eyes reflect the Holy I and lets us know when and how we can come into awareness, without illusion to see clearly. Tzaddi, 90, is the fishhook by which we fill our vessel with mindfulness so we may share ourselves. Quf, 100, is what we seek and why we come to earth. We learn in Quf to separate the stories, tricks and illusions we tell ourselves from the Truth of our Holy connection.

The head gains its ability for expression from the face, as *Quf,* more than any other letter, draws its meaning from the letters around it. Alone, it is a blank, and can not be whole. Thus, *Quf* as in *Kadosh* becomes Wholeness, Holiness.

When *Quf* is joined with *Dalet,* it becomes separate or set apart in a specific way. If we wish to discern that which is holy from the profane, mind and heart must separate. We learn to distinguish what comes from our heart rather than our mind, and thus make mind serve the heart.

At the darkest hour when we feel abandoned, cut off, in fear and trembling, *Quf* is the cry for reunification. Only when lost may we be found. Only when we fall, can we be lifted. At a time when there is nothing left but a fragile hope, nothing we can do but pray, *Quf* is the prayer of the all that is primitive and undeveloped in us calling out from our depths to the Great and Holy. When we who are small, paltry and weak cry out in longing for reunion, our tears open the gates of Heaven. Then, *Quf* is the Holy One sheltering and reaching down in longing for us to acknowledge, welcome, and receive. Mutual longing unites reciprocal energies so that the small and Great, the high and lowly may come together.

Quf is the unexplored territory that draws us. As the back of the head, it is symbolic of the grave or tomb, wherein we have shut up what was too frightening or self-disintegrating to face. It is our shadow, that which we own but do not want to acknowledge. *Quf* is the invitation to know the secret sin with our hopeful prayer for assurance: that even crying out from the grave, our voice is heard. It is the promise of the rainbow. Our brokenness allows us to be made whole, Holy. *Quf,* reassures us that the Holy One is in the still small voice that prays with us as we pray and that makes the whole world Holy. It is the voice of the heart that draws loved ones together. Our existence itself is the result of the divine union of opposites. In this way *Quf* also encompasses the idea of balance.

Quf shares some meanings with the Rider-Waite Tarot card, The Moon. For it can be the *Shekinah,* Feminine Face of God's dark visage, the dark moon, fear in the night, the severe and bitter Tree of Death and the ancient coldness, crying out that we have cut off our own light—Her own light.

REVERSED

When the *Quf* is reversed in a reading, it is because we are in danger of cutting ourselves off from the truth of who we are.

The reversal recommends we ask the difficult questions we've avoided facing:

"What am I trying to hide?"

"What am I hiding from?"

"What am I ignoring?"

"How am I cut off?"

"What is in danger of destruction?"

"What do I need to face up to?"

The whole of creation, the good and bad, superior, and inferior, dark and light, pure and impure, are one. To ignore or attempt to cut off any aspect is to deny Holiness and, ultimately, to self-destruct.

With *Quf* reversed, we need to receive and accept the mirror that presents our own dark face: our severity, our mercilessness, our own tree of death, where we close our ears to Truth. In our dark misery, we learn that even with our wealth of gifts we are helpless.

Feeling lost we call out to the Holy One, who loves, and invites us to love, even our imperfection. Even as we call out to God, God calls out to us. Oneness cannot be without us. Together we are lover and beloved.

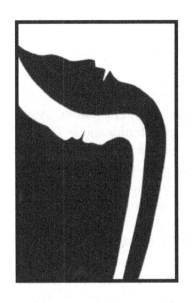 

200 ר *RESH* HEAD FACE COUNTENANCE

Essence: Symbolic of a head *Resh* is the new day dawning, the sun rising and the New Year. It is the Holy One, The Eternal Divine, Mother/Father wholeness. Our hearts rejoice, life renewed. Now in our souls darkness and light dance, and we can know our Self, whole--Holy.

Rider-Waite Tarot: **The Sun**

200 ר *RESH* HEAD FACE
COUNTENANCE

Resh, number 200, signifies the countenance, face or head. *Resh* is the face of the Jewish New Year, *Rosh Hashanah*. As the head of the year it represents both opportunity and fulfillment. At the beginning, joyous union is created, one that may, like the *Song of Songs*, exist on all levels of our being. It may represent the psychic or spiritual union within our Self, or describe the union of beloveds, where two souls are joined, becoming one Love.

Feminine and Masculine, God and *Shekinah*, in *Resh* long to be joined together in us. It is the Eternal joined with Their creation, calling out *Kadosh*, Wholly-ness. "Oh my dove that art in the clefts of the rock, in the secret places of the stars, let me see thy countenance, let me hear thy voice; for sweet is thy voice and thy countenance is comely." (*Solomon's Song*, 2:14)

While Bet, 2, represents a house or womb holding the unborn son, and Kaf, 20, is the hand of the masculine surrounding the small Feminine Yod, Resh, 200, is the new day, the New Year dawning. It is the Femi. nine and Masculine mutual longing and desire that have brought the two together as equals, as One.

Quf, 100, is the dark moon, the darkest hour. The light and promise of Resh, 200, returns once more to bless the earth. Resh and Quf are so related that they can substitute for each other in a reading of a sacred text or oracle deck, depending on context and surrounding letters as words are created

---

When *Resh*, the New Year begins, the gates of heaven open for us to awaken our attention. Like the originally created male and female—Adam, from the first Eden story in Genesis—we are invited to return and live in union with the Eternal in the Eden, here and now, this Earth.

On the Jewish New Year we are offered the opportunity to face ourselves without pretense, to know that we are good and evil, wonderful and hateful. *Resh* is the renewal of all things—the renewal of the creation. Through the movement of our renewed heart, the compassion for the ugly and beautiful in ourselves, we become capable of compassion for others and thus deserving of the Divine Compassion. We can create ourselves anew, recreate our inner harmony and participate in the joy of the new day. Now dancer and dance, singer and song are one and even evil is known to be but the other side of the face of Good. The serpent in Eden was created as a teacher, to offer the freedom of choice. It is through our choices that we learn and grow.

When love is compelled or coerced, it isn't love. Love only exists when it is freely chosen. The Eternal One's gifts of the Serpent and our expulsion from Eden (our infant dependence) are given so that we can choose Love. Without our love and the love of Their creation, the Holy One is incomplete. Without the Holy One's love, we are incomplete. But when two love, God is there.

Resh is similar in meaning to the Rider-Waite Tarot card The Sun. Its image of an Eden where the opposites are united is the two lovers entwined. Wholeness is formed.

REVERSED

When the *Resh* is reversed, it is a sign that we are attempting to coerce or distort ourselves to gain love. There is danger we are living in denial. When we deceive ourselves, deny our true face, we deny our wholeness. This reversal bids us to know and accept our shadow and our light, and truly love ourselves. It warns us that if we are in hiding, how can we hope for or trust anyone else's love for us? Even if it feels wonderful when the object of our love puts us on a pedestal, the love they are offering cannot be real since it is based on an illusion. It is a one-sided reflection, rather than a full view of who we really are. The *Resh* overturned may also indicate we have idealized and not seen the true face of another. Both can lead us into misfortune.

Resh reversed may also signify haughtiness or false pride. We are reminded that when we close the gates of our heart, we shut ourselves out.

300 שׂ שׁ *SHIN* SERPENT'S TOOTH
3RD MOTHER-FIRE

Essence: Symbolic of a serpent's tooth, *Shin* is the fiery serpent Mother, destroyer of illusion. *Shin* first offers us choice, knowledge, power and the ability to be free. Our world explodes awake to a new perceptual paradigm. Our life's meaning is transformed.

  Rider-Waite Tarot: **The Judgment**
  Swiss Tarot: **The Fool**

300 ש שׁ *SHIN* SERPENT'S TOOTH 3RD MOTHER-FIRE

Shin is the number three hundred. It is the symbol of the serpent's tooth. Here in the realm of *Shin*, the fiery serpent offers us the choice of obedience to the Father Protector, who tells us that if we eat of the Tree of the Knowledge of Good and Evil we will die. We can also choose to accept the advice of the wise Mother Serpent who promises us both wisdom and divinity if we eat the fruit. Three times the tree is referred to as the Tree of the Knowledge of Good and Evil, indicating by the use of the word an expression of a non-dualistic Divine reality.

Gimel, 3, is a conduit for the Divine Energy from the heavens, to descend into the world. Lamed, 30, is the illuminating Divine Energy of the world rising up from earth to the heavens. Shin, 300, moves neither solely up nor down, but rather into a wholly new dimension. The merging of the three mothers: Aleph, Mem and Shin, Air, Water and Fire, symbolically come together in Shin to prepare for the birth of Mother Earth, a new form—a new reality. The most difficult questions asked in Quf are answered in Shin.

After our re-creation in Resh (in the garden of double blessing of Genesis I) we find ourselves like Adam and Eve in Genesis II, facing Shin, the fiery serpent mother of birth, death and rebirth. Where Resh is the innocents in the Garden of Eden, Shin is the serpent's entry into a new world.

The Sacred Serpent's bite instantaneously solves all riddles, transporting us to the heart of All Truth. Gimel and Lamed involve movements of the Divine Energy in the dimensions of time and space, whereas Shin refers to a reality existing beyond time and space—a dimension where there is no need for energy to travel from here to there because there is no "there."

In *Shin,* God the Divine Perceiver speaks to us of our mortality when we are one with the masculine aspect of God. The Perceived Mother Serpent offers us immortality in the wisdom of *Shekinah,* the Feminine aspect. Actually Perceived and Perceiver are one. It is the same inseparable Eternal One who in the book of Genesis speaks, saying, "Let Us make Man in Our image and after Our likeness..." that now presents the polarized voices of opportunity.

As the destroyer of illusion, *Shin*'s wisdom encourages us to see our nakedness, surrender our fears and know our true selves. We are both mortal and immortal, male and female, good and evil, yet above all we are whole. The tooth that tears down limitations of form cuts through from one reality to another.

The serpent bite of the *Shin* carries us beyond the materialist idea of reality. We enter the domain of consciousness—of timeless Self where creation and dissolution flow simultaneously, forming, and transforming. For *Shin* is neither animal nor human, neither angelic nor demonic, neither day nor night, but always, *all* ways.

Shin explodes the solid appearance and apparent safety of our world. It is the exalting transformer, awakening us first to our death and aloneness, and then, if we can stand it, to the interweaving Perfection, the experience of *Shema,* (Hearing, to Know God's Unity). In *Shin* we enter the realm where words fail, where all experience vibrates with the radiant Great Mystery. *Shin* involves awakening to a new perceptual paradigm, transforming the context and meaning of our life. The experience of the most intense joy, simultaneously of such terrifying and awesome beauty, moves us to inexpressible realms beyond our normal understanding.

Shin is *Shabbat* (the Sabbath) the creative silence of the heart resting with the Divine, and *shalom,* the peace we make when we live with the consciousness of the multiple unity of ourselves, and God. *Shin* represents the power of three multiplied one hundred times thereby increasing and emphasizing the symbolic power of the triad to both transform and harmonize the opposing forces of duality. The ternary (triad) symbolized by *Shin*, represents the inner structure of The Holy Unity.

The *Shin* is similar to Rider-Waite Tarot card, Judgment and Swiss Tarot card of The Fool. It represents equilibrium, which might last a second or a lifetime. We are balanced rejoicing in the Divine presence. We stand between wisdom and madness. *Shin* is similar to both the Rider-Waite Tarot card, Judgment and the Swiss Tarot card, The Fool, as both involve us being awakened to new-born innocence or reborn into a new perceptual paradigm.

REVERSED

The *Shin* reversed may indicate a lack of balance, or that we have become imbalanced in any number of ways. It could be warning us that we are standing on thin ice. We may feel overwhelmed, flooded with more sensory, psychological or spiritual input than we are able to stand. We may need to develop blinders in order to slow down the flow of input to a level, which we can safely handle.

When our card is reversed, it can indicate a time of clairvoyance or healing crisis. We could be experiencing a time when we are either in or out of our mind, or both simultaneously. In times of great internal transformation, we are advised to insure we maintain our psychological and spiritual equilibrium.

Because *Shin* is joy, laughter, clarity, judgment, and rest, when we cultivate these traits, we can find a way to regain, and maintain, our needed balance.

400 ת ת *TAV* MARK OF PERFECTION
COMPLETION

Essence: Symbolically, mark (of Perfection) in *Tav*, the perfect union of opposites, all forces and energies together, as both completion and beginning anew in a process of perpetual creation. Our lives fill with goodness, compassion, clarity and Truth.

Rider-Waite Tarot: **The World or Universe**

400 ת תּ *TAV* SIGNATURE, SIGN OF PERFECTION   THE WORLD

Tav is the number 400. Because it has two forms, one with the center *Dagesh* (dot) and one without a *Dagesh*, the letter *Tav* encompass the idea of perfection, perpetually beginning and ending only to begin anew. The *Dagesh* in the center of the *Tav* can be seen as the *Aleph (1)*. Thus, the end becomes the beginning.

In the evolution of Tav (400) we begin with Dalet (4), the door through which all life must pass—the Mother perpetually giving birth. Next, in Mem (40) the Mother gives up the child The sacrifice of the mother/child relationship must happen for individuation to occur—so her child can become a man or a woman. Finally, in Tav the lovers have come together as reciprocal co-creators. Tav with the Dagesh is symbolic of the Female and Male of God with their Androgynous child. When Tav (400) is numerologically reduced to 4, it forms the Divine Quaternity expressed in the Divine, unpronounceable Name of God (Yod, Heh, Vav, He), both beginning and completion, which equals the number 8 (The Infinite One).

In Tav, Zayin, (the sword) is reversed to become a support for the Resh (head). Tav is symbolic of perfection: the dynamic union of opposites. Resh is the innocence of the original male/female androgyny, Shin is the new birth process, and Tav is the perfection that we are born from, and into. It is the absolute reciprocal union of male and female, within and without supporting and nourishing one another and, by so doing, joyously and perpetually birthing new creations.

In *Tav*, the desire and longing created by the sword of discernment and order finds fulfillment in union with the fertile and resonant chaos. It is the compassionate harmony, the interpenetration of these two cosmic principles, which allow all meaningful activity to take place. The Feminine Tree of Life and Wisdom rests over the sword, *Zayin*. Now, *Zayin* reversed has become the support for the abundantly productive tree, which is both supported by and supports the sword on which it rests.

In the Genesis of Shin, we were once again given choice, and this time chose the fruit of responsibility, wisdom and non-dualistic unity with the Divine. With Tav, we are given the opportunity to hear the voice of God again and to receive the healed Torah, where the black and white letters swirl in a dance of wondrous delight. The Dagesh in the center of the Tav is the twin-souled baby, the joyous prayer realized, the perfect healing of the Perfection. Tav is the Divine Vessel again whole and once more containing the light of the Infinite Divine compassion.

Now, in a process of perpetual, perfecting creation, all aspects dance together. The completion of *Tav* provides us with the openness and clarity to live with the order in chaos, and with the chaos in order. Here is spontaneous joy that allows us to follow the path of our Heart. All aspects of life dance together and we are capable of living to our potential. Now, in spite of our fears, we can live with full participation in a paradoxical world, even if we never receive final answers to the mystery and meaning of our existence. Without ultimate guarantees, we nevertheless have developed our ability to love. By so doing, we appreciate the miraculous sacredness of all life.

Tav shares some meaning with the Rider-Waite Tarot, World or Universe card.

Tav is a card of goodness, activity, openness, of perpetual newness and compassion, of self-integration and growth.

REVERSED

When *Tav* is reversed it's a warning not to throw oneself away on the world through impatience and possessiveness. The attitude, "I want it all and I want it now!" cannot help but throw us back into a state of illusion and grief.

We are at risk of losing what we have journeyed so far to gain. *Tav* reversed might describe a situation similar to the story of the fisherman's wife, who went from satisfaction to desiring and receiving more and more until at last she was thrown back into the poverty from which she had come, and in some sense had never left.

A LOOK AT THE RELATIONSHIPS BETWEEN HEBREW LETTERS SHARING THE SAME NUMEROLOGICAL ROOT

1 א In *Aleph*, the chaos is expansive, full of all potential. It encompasses all that exists and all that might ever exist. Even nothingness exists within the One. It is the one to which all are trying to evolve. The *Aleph* in its silent potential, about to exhale into a becoming of sound, is a symbol of God's capacity for outwardly creative movement. It is the macrocosm.

10 י The *Yod* is the reverse capacity. It is the image of the monad, the microcosm, an inhalation toward its specific, smallest center. The expansion of the *Aleph* has completed its outward movement and, with *Yod,* has begun to contract toward its inward potential.

100 ק *Quf* is the prayer for the joining of opposites in one movement; the inseparable, interacting, and everlasting desire of each for the other. *Quf* is also the fulfillment of crying out to the Divine and the Divine answering. The small and great drawing together to become One Love.

2 ב ב *Bet* is the beginning of creation; first Herself empty, then Herself as the Mother as She creates within her encircling body the son-seed, first creation.

20 ךכב The *Kaf* is the *Bet* inside out as it evolves. The empty hand of the created, the ephemeral fingers of the Son, await the Eternal. Then, *Kaf* with the *Dagesh* is the Eternal Female surrounded by the Male, Her creation. Finally, it is the hand closed tight.

200 ר In the *Resh*, Female and Male are merged. They are no longer a union of opposites. They have become one, a new form, free to choose their new day, symbolized by the face of the sun.

3 ג ﬞ *Gimel* is the conduit for Divine energy as it comes to manifest in the   physical world.

30 ל *Lamed* is the channel for the illuminating energy of the earth. The world is enlightened and rises up toward Heaven.

300 ש שׁ With *Shin*, energy moves neither up nor down but rather into a new dimension. *Shin* symbolizes the instantaneous and spontaneous movement of energy between worlds. In *Shin*, there is no here or there, just Being. As the third Mother, Fire, *Shin,* evaporates the Water of *Mem* into Air, *Aleph*. The merging of the three, Air, Water and Fire, can then birth Earth, a new form

4 ד   *Dalet* is the door through which all life must pass. She is the Mother perpetually giving birth and the child always being born.

40 מם *Mem* is the Mother giving up the child, and the child giving up the Mother. It is the sacrifice necessary for individuation to occur, so that he may grow and choose to come together with the Mother again, to perpetuate the creation of all life. She is Water, Mother nature and the preserver of life.

400 תﬞ In *Tav*, The lovers finally come together, Male and Female, God and Goddess, Equal, reciprocal partners and co-creators. The *Tav* with the *Dagesh* is symbolic of the Mother-Goddess, Father-God, and the Androgynous Divine-Child of their creating. The Trinity, in its potential of continued and continual creation, is also, paradoxically, The Quaternity within the One, *Yod, Heh, Vav, Heh,* Holy Name.

5 ה *Heh* is the wind-door through which the breath of life flows. It is the beginning of the male God's individuation. It is Love, looking out the window at his Beloved.

50 בַ The *Nun* is the dual form of the soul in its original state before being born. Nun swims between worlds; *Nun* is the love of the soul for its other half.

6 וו *Vav* is the link joining opposites, the bridge, the linking of high and low. It is a sign   of communion moving toward completion.

60 ס The *Samekh* is the joining *Vav* coming full cycle. It not only links high and low, but in coming to meet itself, it encircles as well as unites all experience, becoming circumspect. Yet viewed as a spiral, it only ends for a new beginning to emerge.

7 ז *Zayin* is the sword, which by dividing creates the urge to unite. It is the ability to discern and to choose.

70 ע *Ayin* is the eye, which is capable of division, of discriminating between appearances. It can be vulnerable to being fooled by appearances; then, the divisions it creates may prevent rather than inspire unification.

8 ח *Chet* is what we choose to be responsible for. It is whatever we claim as our own, what we surround or enclose. *Chet* is the marriage canopy and that which we pledge ourselves to.

80 ףפ *Pe* is the mouth that makes the pledge. *Pe* is our words by which we state a claim or make a vow. It is the words we use to define the nature of that which we call reality. It is how we express our values and how we frame our thoughts or feelings. *Pe* is where we become lost and entangled, or find ourselves.

9 ט *Tet* is the sign of resistance and protection. As the final single digit in the *Aleph-Bet*, it is the Serpent Goddess of Wisdom and inspiration. She offers the knowledge of good and evil and is the giver of immortality.

90 ץצ *Tzaddi* in its multiple relationship to *Tet, 9,* is related by extension to all ideas of term, solution, purpose, and goal.

It symbolizes the deeds of giving, of the good received from the source shared with others, for it is through sharing our gifts that the Divine enters the world.

THE HOLY NAME INFORMS
THE STRUCTURE OF MY TAROT DECK

י

ה

ו

ה

The structure of my Tarot deck reflects the four levels of manifestation inherent in what the sages refer to as "The Divine name of the Tetragrammaton." At the top the *Yod* represents the as yet unrealized Divine will, which nevertheless contains the germ of the Entirety. It is the black fire on white fire of the card backs. The letters, which form the Major Arcana, represent the first *Heh*, world of Divine Creation, since it was through letters that creation occurred. The number cards (one through ten) represent the *Vav*, water of emotion, the divine forming energy of the ten Sefirot, each one containing universes. In the final *Heh*, the face card's realistic images contain elements of all the previous levels, since they are representative of the world of action. The structure and arrangement of my cards involves the most realistic-appearing element actually being most transitory and ephemeral element of reality. They are faces seen in the mirror of time, illusions of personality, shards of the divine vessel, that yet contain in their depths the light of the Eternal.

The Holy Name consists of four letters adding up (numerologically) to 8, the signifier of infinity. The Name may also be read as a *Yod* (10=1) plus two times *Resh* (200=400 or 4) plus three times *Vav* (6=18=9). All these (1 plus 4 plus 9) equals 14 which reduces to 5.

The number 5 is the letter "He" or wind-door through which

the Divine breath enters us. And then, filled with the Divine Breath as the *Heh* (formed by a *Resh* 200, or 2, and a *Vav* 6), we become 8 and are one with Infinite Being.

THE DIVINE NAME

According to Jewish tradition, one must never pronounce The Most Holy Name of

God. The reason given for this custom is that The Name is too sacred to be spoken aloud. To speak the Name would diminish the greatness of its meaning.

There is no absolute information concerning the origin of The Holy Name. The original interpretation of the יהוה has also been lost in the thousands of years since its inception. Only the Kabbalistic writings, which appeared long after the appearance of the earliest Torah, attempted to explain the symbolic meaning of the Name.

The Kabbalists envisioned the four letter/numbers in the Name as referring to the four worlds of creation. They also perceived The Name as referring to a unity containing within itself the *Yod* (י) Father, *Heh* (ה)Mother, *Vav* (ו) Son, and *Heh* (ה)Daughter. Thus, it is within the tradition to consider the possibility that each letter of THE NAME is actually an initial of an attribute or aspect of THE ONE.

I believe the original meaning of The Name had primarily maternal rather than paternal order. The maternal order better reflects the symbolism of the individual letters that compose The Name. The wisdom of the letters from their pre-patriarchal forms can still be seen as they presently appear. To begin, the *Yod* (י) is pictograph of a finger or hand and was associated with the Great Goddess, called She Who Shapes Life Like a Pot.

The One who creates human beings from clay in the Hebrew scriptures was originally the Great Goddess of the Sumerian and Babylonian creation myths. The *Heh* (ה), symbolizing a wind-door or window, refers to that opening through which Being, spirit, soul, air or wind enters and leaves. *Vav* (ו) symbolizes a hook or nail, which fastens one thing to another. It is the joiner of opposites, that which transforms and gives continuity. It is the first letter of the word penis, that body part which joins male and female into one being so that they may create together. Thus, *Vav* represents God

The Father side of The Creator, followed by the final *Heh* (ה) completes the spiral of Creation of Divine Being and the wind-door. It is through this door which God moves from Divine Unity into the material world of infinite creations and multiple worlds, including the paradise of Genesis, as well as our present one.

Hebrew is a language in which gender is always indicated by the letter ending of words. The ה , *Heh,* and ת , *Tov* are feminine endings. All other final letters indicate the masculine. However, the letter ה at the end of a word can occasionally be masculine. This change of gender is determined by the vowel mark for the letter preceding the *Heh* at the end of a word. The lack of such a mark indicates the Divine Name most likely (but not necessarily) has a Feminine ending.

Therefore, יהוה The Divine name is not definitively masculine nor feminine. It is the only singular pronoun in Hebrew that does not connote male or female, but both and more. In the first verse of Genesis, God refers to God-Self in the plural saying, "Let Us create man in our image after our likeness…" (*Genesis* 26) God then creates male and female in God's image. Since, from the earliest record, יהוה the unpronounceable and therefore untranslatable Holy Name of God does not contain a vowel mark in conjunction with the letter *Vav*, so the Name is simultaneously female and male, androgynous, gender-free and more. It is the original "Royal We."

TREE OF LIFE

The planetary correspondences by this author, match the meaning of the *Sefirot* better than the traditional, androcentric and patriarchal ones

KETAR
Holy ONE
Will, the edge of the void, the Divine Name, "I Shall Be What I Will Be", Source, first emanation, and ultimate return.
(Neptune)

BINAH
Understanding, reason, receptive capacity, thought, the beginning of form.
(Mercury)

HOKHMAH
Wisdom, the active intellect. Flash of genus, or inspiration, Revelation, awareness. Mental energy
(Uranus)

DAAT
The Holy Spirit, the non-Sefirot, instantaneous knowing of God, where the Absolute may enter at will.
(Pluto)

GEVURAH
Severity, contraction, limitation, structuring, and testing, passive emotion, fear of God
control, strength, judgment, discipline, rigor.
(Saturn)

TIFERET
Beauty, compassion, harmonizing principal beween the forces of infinite expansion and infinite contraction. Beauty we understand. Mingling of thought with love. Love given form, the Heart of hearts, essence of Love. Celebration of life.
(Venus)

HESED
Expansiveness, chaos, mercy, Active emotion, opening-out, generosity, love of God, power, greatness tolerance, emotion of love, emanation.
(Jupiter)

HOD
Reverberation, majesty Passive, cognitive, controlling, responsive, splendor, passive, authority, reflective, theorizing, measure, multiplication, responses. Awesome beauty that's beyond understanding.
(Sun)

YESOD
Foundation, formation, the generative element, root of all that is, ego, center of marrow, sap, and power, the organs of generation through which the procreative vitality flows.
(Mars)

NETZACH
Eternity, lasting, endurance, fixity, instinctive, and impulsive, practice, contemplation, victory, active repose, force, desires, will.
(Moon)

MALKHUT
The Divine Presence in matter, the material world, the dominion of the Divine Feminine. Matter in every form. All of creation, the earth, the body.
(Earth)

TREE OF LIFE

The planetary correspondences by this author, match the meaning of the *Sefirot* better than the traditional,
androcentric and patriarchal ones

DYNAMIC MOGEN DAVID TREE OF LIFE SEFIROT
INCLUDING THE DAAT
A fractal pattern expanding infinitely in and out

THE SEFIROTIC TREE OF LIFE'S
RELATIONSHIP
TO THE TAROT SUITS

This section explores the meaning of the ten *Sefirot* plus the *Daat,* their positions on the Tree of life, and a description of the four suits of the Minor Arcana.

I've kept my images of the numbered cards of the Minor Arcana consistent with their placement on the Tree of Life *(Sefirotic Tree).* The ten positions of the Divine attributes appearing on the *Sefirotic* tree have been at the center of Kabbalistic thought throughout its existence. Although the Tree has been diagrammed in various ways throughout its long history, with the exception of the Aces, the most common *Sefirotic* placements are used for all my numbered card illustrations.

The Aces, being first as *Ketar*, encompass the potential of the whole. Each Ace therefore holds the *Ketar* position (Tree of Life) of a particular realm of action, illustrated by its individual suit.

From the twos on, I have maintained the numbers' positions as *Sefirot* on the Tree of Life. The position of the ten *Sefirot* on the Tree is essential to the understanding of their meaning.

For example: While two *Sefirot* placed side by side appear to indicate balance, the second *Sefirot's* position on the Tree of Life appears imbalanced, as the second image appears to be falling away from the central One.

Ketar, position One on the Tree of Life, represents the Totality, the Infinite One complete in itself. Called the *En Sof*, it means Eternal Source, from which all comes and must in the end return, propelled by its dance. *Ketar,* One, contains the multitudinous potential for manifestation.

Yet this One must divide itself momentarily to create the inspired dancing partner called *Hokhmah* (Wisdom).

This second *Sefirot, Hokhmah* (Wisdom) is caught and balanced by the third *Sefirot, Binah* (Understanding). The three form the triangle of potential: *Ketar*, Eternal Source, *Hokhmah,*

Wisdom *and Binah*, Understanding. These three circle through the invisible non-*Sefirot Daat.* Knowing that they are simultaneously complete and incomplete. They lack any manifestation.

And so the fourth is born. Although the number four in Western thought connotes stability, in many writings on numerology, the fourth, *Hesed,* position on the Tree is expressive of not only Love, but expansive energy, emotion and a rush toward unlimited expansion, the antithesis of stability.

The four directions, East, West, South, and North, are here, but not up or down, Inside or Outside. The stability of the four is an illusion, something seen very one-dimensionally.

Though with the five, *Gevurah* (Severity, Restriction, Contraction), the image is more balanced it is still incomplete. Now the four directions, East, South, West and North plus Up, are in place, but the image looks like a rocket. It is still open at the bottom waiting for Down, to complete the circle.

The sixth direction, *Tiferet* (Compassion, Love in action, Acts of Loving Kindness) forms the grounding downward reach, that balance which incorporates the totality of the whole. The *Sefirot* now form a circle creating a boundary between the visible and invisible realms. *Tiferet's* circle of compassion holds the six pointed Star of David or *Mogen David.* This configuration reflects the potential of the whole tree, yet is still not it. *Tiferet* is the paradox of being both complete and incomplete. The completion must still, in order to realize itself as the *En Sof* (One), must create the mirrored pool wherein its light and darkness can be reflected and expand.

In the seventh position, *Netzach* (Eternity) God is viewing creation. The One rests outside the creation, viewing the work. This again unbalances the whole and by its weight, sets the circle spinning again. The seventh one is a pause to rest between ending and beginning. It is the *Shabbat,* waiting to enter and be entered, as we wait for the *Shekinah* to arrive. The rest after creation is an active rest, the contemplation of eternity cannot become stagnant and so forces all to go on.

The seventh position creates a need for balance, which leads to the eighth position, *Hod* (Glory, Reverberation). Once more, the tree appears to be stable, balanced by the forces of Eternity and Reverberation. Yet, like a rocket in shape, it is still ungrounded.

Something is still missing; the mirror is still incomplete, a tree of branches, but without root or trunk. A foundation or trunk is needed: *Yesod* (Foundation) becomes the means by which we are able to join ourselves to the whole.

*Yesod i*s the serpent coiled around the tree trunk, offering us the means by which we may become not only the mirror of God, but the realization that we are not separate from God. God is both mirror and mirrored, since all our existence is cast in the image of the Divine.

The serpent coils about the trunk of the tree tempting us to self-knowledge. In the tenth *Sefirot* position, *Malkhut* (World of manifestation, where *Shekinah* enters and dwells), we enter the body, the root of The Tree. This is the world of manifestation, capable of reflecting in the tiniest portion of each cell, the holographic view of the complete mirror, infinitely and completely mirroring itself.

THE FOUR SUITS OF THE MINOR ARCANA

The four suits of the Minor Arcana:

Wands, the fire suit of inspiration and the potential of creation

Cups, water, the suit of emotion

Swords, air, thought

Wheels, earth

The way these interdependent suits function can be illustrated, employing music as an example. Wands represent the existence and potential of music. Cups are the desire to express the overflow of emotion to which music owes its existence. Swords represent the ability to imagine the structure and sound you want to create and the ability to choose a piece that would best express the appropriate emotion. Wheels are the realm of the instrument, the ability to actually play and make music. All four necessary stages are manifest aspects of the whole.

In keeping with the aim of making a deck wherein the dark and light dance with equal energy, I alternated between light-on-dark backgrounds and dark-on-light backgrounds when designing the suits.

Each suit offers insights into any or all relationships or areas of experience within the realm symbolized by that suit. For example, Cups represent the water of emotion and therefore are applicable to all intimate relationships. Although the relationships described in the cups suit are those that have to do with love, lovers and the love that binds people together to create a family, their meaning can be extended to include all close relationships. The evolution of one kind of relationship can be generalized to all significant emotional relationships. The context and intensity may differ, but the general dynamics and developmental signposts are often the same.

Cups, when applied to work relationships, might move from the *Binah* of finding the perfect job, boss, work, partnership, etc. to the *Hesed* of feeling taken for granted, to the *Gevurah* of bucking or challenging the system, questioning a practice, asking for a raise.

Likewise, when we apply the information to parent/child relationships, it might go from the *Ketar*, the ability to have a child, to *Hokhmah,* the desire for one, to *Binah,* that love at first sight when the baby arrives, to the *Hesed* of taking it home and then losing oneself in the care-taking and emotional demands of parenting, to the *Gevurah* of pulling back from the state of total absorption to reassert our own needs, to the *Tiferet,* the compassionate rebalancing of the relationship.

The same process may be applied to friendships or significant teacher-student relationships.

In order to know which relationship the cards in a reading are referring to, it is helpful to examine the surrounding cards and the context of the reading as a whole. For example, if the surrounding cards are wheels, it might indicate a work relationship; if wands, the cup card could be describing a relationship with a teacher or spiritual guide.

A JUNGIAN VIEW OF THE TAROT SUITS

It is also useful to view the four Tarot suits through the lens provided by the work by Carl Jung and his followers on Personality Types, the face cards can be interpreted and understood as follows:

Wands are the Intuitive-Perceptive types

Cups are Feeling-Perceptive types

Swords are Thinking-Judging types

Wheels are the Sensate-Judging types

All four Types may be predominantly Introverted or Extroverted.

For the last suit, I chose the image of Wheels (or, in one deck, Pizzas) because of their vital cyclical qualities. The Wheels suit, where the *Sefirot* descend to earth, also reflects the Wheel Ezekiel saw, which has often been associated with the *Sefirot* on the Tree of Life.

The Queens lead the court cards of the Wands and Cups suits. Wands are the realm of origins and inspiration. It is the initial impulse of creation housed in the dark, secret, all-encompassing depths of the Feminine. The Wands suit is drawn from the black fire, the primordial chaos, the Great Womb of Creation and Original Essence from which all proceeds. The Cups suit represents the realm of the water of life. It is the light side of the Feminine where all creation is nourished through the bright web, the binding and interweaving of the myriad relationships that compose the Whole.

The Kings lead the Swords and Wheels suits. The Swords are the suit of thought and discerning mentality. Wheels is also led by a King. It represents the world we live in, which is still controlled by patriarchal values. The last card of the Wheels suit, however, and of the entire deck, is the Princess of Wheels, who personifies a coming change.

Face cards in a reading are significant in determining the qualities of the person of interest in the relationship.

The final face card in each suit, as the youngest, may refer either to a child or young person. The Infant of Wheels, for example, might easily refer to the relationship between the questioner and an infant or young child. Or, the last face card in each suit may refer to a message arriving. The type of message will relate to the realm ruled by the suit the face card represents. For example: a message of an emotional nature or communication from a loved one would be represented by the Prince of Cups. A legal message such as a legal document or summons would be likely be represented by the Princess of Swords.

REGARDING THE ARCHETYPES REPRESENTED IN THE FACE CARDS

Like the archetypes expressed in the Hebrew letters, the archetypes described by the face cards exist within and outside of us regardless of age and even gender. Thus, whatever our gender, each of us contains within us, and express at various times and to varying degrees, both the male and female archetypes represented by the face cards.

The personas represented by these archetypes, some more than others and at varying times in our lives, reflect the different aspects of our conscious and unconscious selves. This is most easily understood when we consider all the characters who fill our dreams as well as people we see in our waking lives.

THE MINOR ARCANAS NUMBERED CARDS

RELATIONSHIP TO THE SEFIROTIC TREE OF LIFE

So that we need not continually look up the individual meanings of Minor Arcana cards during a reading, I have summarized the ten cards that accompany the royalty. These may be interpreted more easily if we keep in mind the context of the individual suits: Wands = creative/inspiration,

Cups = emotions/relationships and feeling states, Swords = thinking. Wheels = the worldly realm where all three come together

KETAR, Crown: The Aces represent totality, the one complete in itself. It is Source, and the will to become manifest.

HOKHMAH, Wisdom: Twos represent an initial awareness of separation and a desire for union.

BINAH, Understanding: Threes represent the triangle, an apparent completion that is actually a beginning. It is a circling of energy before manifestation, simultaneously complete and incomplete.

HESED, Expansion, or Emotional Love, Chaos: Fours represent an expansion of energy, an opening out, expressing a need for a state of stability/balance.

GEVURAH, Judgment, or Severity: Fives represent a contraction of energy, solidifying force.

TIFERET, Beauty, Compassion, Love: Sixes represent the completion of a cycle, the balancing of energies, the paradox of being both complete and incomplete. It is the culmination of the world of creation, the center of the world of formation, and the beginning of the world of action.

NETZACH, Eternity: Sevens represent the pause between ending and beginning, waiting to enter and/or be entered, a time for contemplation.

HOD, Reverberation: The eights represent a time of increased activity, where demands are made by the world we have chosen as our own.

YESOD, Foundation: Nines represent the means by which we are able to join ourselves to the whole, the serpent coiled around the trunk of the tree tempting us to either self-knowledge or destruction.

MALKHUT, World (material world): The tens represent both the culmination of the energy where it is grounded and the transformation as it becomes mirror, mirrored, a new beginning.

THE SYMBOLISM IN THE DESIGN OF THE WANDS SUIT

Wands, the first of the four suits reflects the *Yod* energy of the *Tetragrammaton* (four letter name of God) *Yod Heh Vav Heh*. This first suit has an arboreal and spiritual connection which links it to the Tree of Life. *Yod*, being also the number 10, evokes the ten Sefirot which compose the Tree of Life.

The image of an open flower represents the receptive inspirational nature of this suit. The salamander represents the element of fire, for the wands suit is about being open and receptive to the creative, transformative fire of inspiration.

Wands are the suit of inspiration, creativity, and connection to the primary state of the divinity; the one, ten, and all and no thing; the monad that incorporates the information of the whole.

KETAR, ACE OF WANDS

Essence: Ketar of wands embraces the essence and potential of the Wands suit. Gifted. Intuition led. Connection to Source. Creative or spiritual energy and potential--the initiating impulse and beginning of all creative efforts.

    The Ace, Ketar of Wands represents the path of the spirit. Spirit here refers to the intersection where our finite mind is one with the conscious universe. This first card of the Wands suit contains the inherent capacities: spirit, energy, inspiration and source simultaneously; intuition, expansiveness, warmth of fire, and the ability for creative expression. The Ketar of Wands will always express potential for spiritual growth. It indicates the beginning of a spiritual or creative enterprise and the connection to the Source of inspiration. We are full of creative potential and eager for participating in its manifestation. This represents a conception, which may manifest on a spiritual or physical plane.
    Listen to your dreams. Invisible to all but our own selves,

omnipresent, dreams are our guide to self-understanding and growth, a potential source of spiritual learning and prophecy, and one important path of the Holy Spirit.

Ketar of Wands symbolizes the initiation of Creative Energy we may invite, invoke, wait for, anticipate, play with, ascend and aspire to. It can never be forced and enters only when we are empty to receive it.

REVERSED

The Ketar of Wands as stated above will always express potential for spiritual growth. However, when reversed it may even refer to a physical conception, in which case it may mean a new being will enter our life through whom a spiritual lesson or realization is experienced. It may indicate inspiration manifesting in or relating to our body or need for movement in our physical world, a new approach to diet, health or travel. It may even indicate the conception of a child who has incarnated so that we may learn important spiritual lessons.

If we are feeling uninspired the Ketar of Wands reversed suggests we ensure our physical, spiritual or emotional energy is not blocked. When we release the binding chains of fear, shame, self-consciousness, and doubt, our senses, intuition and emotions become open and receptive. Our freed energy guides and connects us to our Creative Source so we may fulfill our highest potential.

2 HOKHMAH OF WANDS

Essence: Reflection and receptivity. We may experience conflict between our initial inspiration and the work required if we wish to manifest the full expression of that which originally inspired us. We wonder if it is worth the effort.

The *Hokhmah* (Two) of Wands represents a state of division or internal conflict between our initial inspiration and the energy that it takes to manifest it. There may be an apparent divergence from the source of our inspiration. This is a time for gaining perspective, a time for reflecting on our conflicting and paradoxical perceptions. These conflicts can, if we are receptive, lead toward spiritual growth, greater understanding and a higher level of integration. To dream is easy. To manifest the dream requires work, patience, and persistence.

We may be feeling separated from our source of inspiration. If this is the case, it is important to realize that this separation can be useful. It allows us the opportunity to evaluate our inspiration in order to know if its pursuit would be the best use of our energy or if it would it be better to wait. With the Two of Wands, we have left the womb, the source of creativity, the center of security. The sheltering world of our dreams and fantasies has not been left easily, but with fear and trembling, and yet, in this process, we are already participating in the beginning of our own creation. It is the beginning of individuation, the beginning of responsibility for our own creative process.

REVERSED

If reversed, the *Hokhmah* of Wands card could indicate a failure of observation and a danger of self-delusion, empty dreams of glory, an unconsidered following of an idea we take as inspiration without being aware of its source or potential demands.

This is the time for questioning our initial impulse. We need to ask, "Does this idea represent our best choice or focus for our energy? Or is it simply the first result of a brainstorm?"

"What steps will this process require?"

"How much time or sacrifice might be necessary to make my idea a reality?"

This reversal may also indicate an unwillingness to wake up from the dream. The time has come to quit our unnecessary clinging to the past and move on.

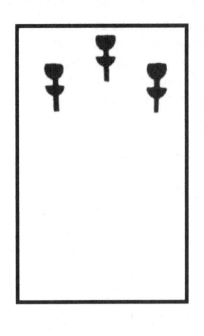

3 BINAH OF WANDS

Essence: Understanding. Wisdom and intuition unite. We are filled with Joyousness and pregnant expectation as we commit to following our Source Inspiration. Now even our dreams may carry teaching messages and guidance to assist our purpose.

In the *Binah* (three) of Wands, intuition and inspiration are united with the Source energy. The *Binah* of Wands brings understanding, perspective, resolution and spiritual growth. The source of creative self-expression is joined to wisdom and intuition. We experience an easy flow of creative energy. We are joyful. Life feels connected and meaningful. In the *Binah* we are filled with energy of the Creative. We are aflame, exultant and passionately alive. This card can be indicative of a pregnant state, either literal or metaphoric, since it represents the containment and nourishing of creative energy. It is a time of inner growth. There is no need to immediately push ourselves to produce an outer manifestation or expression. To do so would be premature. Our dreams now have great meaning and often beauty. They may be prophetic, revealing either mysteries of the cosmos or else giving great personal insights or both. This can be a good time for journaling or sketching. It is time to create an outline or container for what is to become.

REVERSED

When reversed the *Binah* of Wands remains virtually unchanged. However, it is a reminder we need to listen deeply and learn to pay extra attention to our internal processes. We need to give ourselves space to experience the pregnancy fully. This is a time to dream, to nourish ourselves and trust in the growth of the seed within. It is a time to gestate, relax and tune in.

Although in reversed position, we may feel that everything is moving too slowly, there is no urgency for us to strive after anything. If we feel irritated or impatient and restless it only wastes our energy and can make us unhappy. Here we are required to remain open with a listening heart, and when we ready for that for which we wait, it will come.

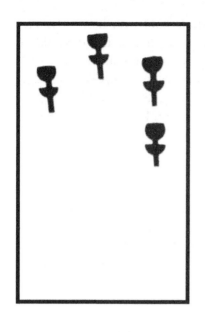 

4 HESED OF WANDS

Essence: Excitement. Exultation. Creative or spiritual
expansiveness can lead us to become lost in inspiration.
Everything flows and contributes as we are totally absorbed and
one with our purpose.

The *Hesed* (four) of Wands indicates a time of creative
and/or spiritual expansiveness and expression. We may become
so attuned to the expansiveness of God's love and immersed in
our creative flow, that we lose the necessary awareness of our
physical needs.

Carried away and lost in inspiration, we may forget to eat,
lose track of our belongings or ignore our responsibilities.
There may be feelings of tremendous exultation and
excitement. We may become so merged with the Source and its
expression that we lose track of what we are actually intending
to create.

Where this usually wouldn't be a good thing, at this time our total immersion can lead us to making creative accidents which can result in wonderful and unexpected directions. This state is essential for any creative work.

Although we may be temporarily unbalanced we will eventually come back, either through our own energy swings or from recognizing that we need to ask assistance, a helper, possibly even someone who will help keep track of our material or physical needs.

Make the most of this time of creative expansiveness and inspiration. It is important to realize that it will not last. If there is anything uninspired to do, get it done fast, get a helper or put it off until later.

REVERSED

If reversed, *Hesed* of Wands warns that we are in danger of flying off into the spacious fantasy of our creative ecstasy. In the upside down of *Hesed,* we have over-expanded our imaginings and are becoming lost to the reality that we will eventually be required to return into balance so as to actually produce what we have been inspired to create.

We are also required to attend to our own physical existence and its demands. Our health or the health of our relationships is endangered if we neglect the demands and responsibilities imposed by our physical reality.

Even when almost all our energy is focused on the birth process and creative outpouring, we nevertheless do need to take care of our relationships and those things which are absolutely necessary for survival.

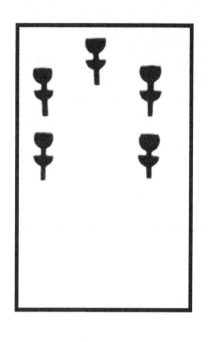

5 GEVURAH OF WANDS

Essence: Feeling uninspired and disconnected from Source. The well is dry. Life may seem routine, repetitive, meaningless. Our energy seems to have suddenly drained away. We question our original idea and wonder if our faith was misplaced.

The *Gevurah* (five) of Wands may be indicative of a time when we are feeling uninspired; the well is dry and we feel disconnected from Source. Where previously we were completely immersed in the creative process, we now experience a sense of loss. We feel constricted and question the meaning or direction in our life. There is a sense that the magic we originally experienced is gone, and we fear it may never return. Life seems routine and repetitious.

The five of Wands may indicate a time when we are physically or psychically drained. It may be an indication that the physical demands of our body or environment weigh too heavily upon us.

This is a signal that what's important now is to take care of the mundane and all that was ignored or left unfinished when we were fully engaged in our creative process. It's time to come back down to earth. We need to face the fact that that which in the throes of inspiration was neglected now requires care.

This distress we experience is but a sign of the times, the other side of the same creative process. It is important to remember that this experience of postpartum depression is simply the flip side of our creative process. The earlier experience of expansiveness and immersion required this time of felt constriction for balance, for rest.

All that is to be done is to wait out the bad time and persevere in acting as though the inspiration is there so as not to lose track or focus. Then, when the energy changes, we are able to return again to an even richer creative expression.

REVERSED

When the *Gevurah* of Wands is reversed, the dry time we feel stuck in may be of longer duration or our experience of depressed and constricted energies are felt more intensely. It is possible that our blocked energy has a psychological source that we need to work through or come to terms with in order for any change in our situation to occur. It might be a signal that we can't do it all alone and therefore should look outside ourselves for help and new sources of inspiration.

In doing so, we must nevertheless be careful that in our vulnerability we don't allow ourselves to be dominated by others' values. These can only carry us further from our source and lead us to conform or imitate. This is a time to examine the way fear and the desire for security makes us distrust our creative impulses or intuition. If we wish to restore our ability to live creatively, even when looking outside ourselves for assistance and inspiration, we need to remain attentive to our inner truth and trust our own reality.

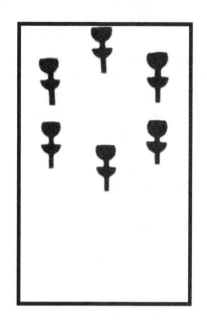 

6 TIFERET OF WANDS

Essence: Equilibrium is attained. Our creative work and personal life flows effortlessly. Even so we must stay awake to unforeseen pitfalls that may undermine our project. There's a necessity for vigilance and attention to detail as the time of transition nears completion.

The *Tiferet* (six) of Wands refers to a time when the transition from the old to the new is nearing completion. The forces that usually tended in different directions are harmonized. It is a time of perfect equilibrium. In principle, everything is where it belongs and proceeds as if without effort. It can be tempting to complacently drift along and let things take their course. Just as in the Genesis story when, following the creation of the world, the serpent appears with its potential for enlightening or for throwing all into chaos or death, it is most important to remain awake and vigilant *even* to seemingly insignificant details.

Hence, the *Tiferet* of Wands refers to a time of completion, enjoyment, harmonious relationships. Simultaneously, it is a time for remaining alert. With self-awareness and internal watchfulness, the seemingly insignificant evil will not go unnoticed. We must avoid becoming complacent, conditioned, or habitual. The times now require us to remain awake and vigilant, regarding our internal processes even as the external aspects of our life appear to have reached a state of harmony. We must remain humble, orderly, grounded, responsible, awake and watchful. Resist the temptation to impulsivity, carelessness or simply drifting along.

REVERSED

When reversed, the meaning of the *Tiferet* of Wands is essentially the same, but we are more vulnerable to the dangers of complacency. Habitual ways of thinking and being, also our addiction to comforts are symptomatic of mental stagnation and its resulting dangers.

This reversal invites us to question our motives and ask, "Is my work here really as good as it can be?"

"Am I too anxious to be finished?"

"What might I be forgetting or leaving out? Is any step in my process incomplete?"

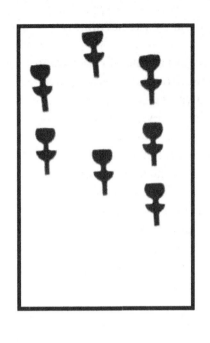

7 NETZACH OF WANDS

Essence: Love and joy as we allow ourselves to delight in our perception of the Holy Sacred world. Here, we know that our sense of purpose and the blessings we experience are a reflection of our connection to Source.

The heart must be joined to our inspiration for anything meaningful to be created. The *Netzach* of Wands indicates a time of pleasure, allowing the emotions to flow. We are reminded that, rather than escapes, fascinations and the accumulation of stuff, it is love and joy, physical pleasure and the myriad offerings of the natural world that give the product of our inspiration meaning. We trust that our experience of depth and awareness of meaning in our life is not a trick or gimmick, but a true expression of our connection to Source. We are a child of the universe, a lover in the dance and dancer in the love celebration of God and life.

It is as though a curtain has been lifted. Suddenly the world burns with a crystalline brilliance; at that moment of intensity we know our limits, the precious fragility of life, but nevertheless we experience the joyful, the infinite/eternal encounter with the divine.

Our heart opens. Flooded by an awareness of our connection to the most radiant and incomprehensible beauty we feel a passionate sense of deep meaning and connection to Infinite Source.

REVERSED

When the *Netzach* of Wands is reversed we are on autopilot and no longer fully present. If we find ourselves feeling cut off or out of touch it may be a sign we need to cultivate a more joyful and loving attitude, to expand our concern from our self to an other. When we can find one thing for which to be grateful, it can help us reconnect with the absolute miracle and privilege of this gift of life.

Joy and pleasure in life can't depend on external circumstances. Instead they depend on our own awareness. Stories filled with appreciation for the Eternal and Life have come even from those who under the most horrific conditions, surrounded by cruelty and devastation, were still able to transcend their suffering, and find beyond their pain a purpose, even gratitude and a reason to live another day.

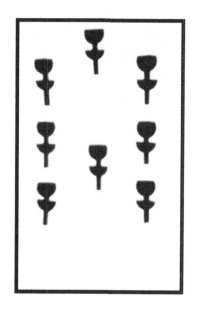
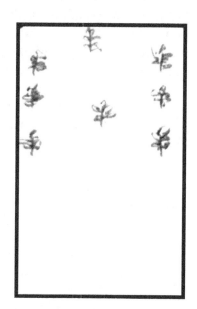

8 HOD OF WANDS

Essence: We've learned to trust our Divine Guidance. Time to act on and exemplify our newfound awareness. Take a risk, change direction. Now we need to review our creation and decide if it's working or not. The wisest choice may sometimes be to tear up our lovely page for the good of the whole.

The *Hod* (eight) of Wands says that, having had rest and the chance for reflection and gratitude (as required by the *Netzach* of Wands), the time now demands we act. It is time to live fully with the lesson of faith, to practice, work and exemplify our new awareness. We are called to risk ourselves yet have faith in the invisible. It is important to trust in our vision, even if this trust goes counter to all our rationality.

Though coupled with feelings of fear, there is a great potential for spiritual growth here. We leap like divers into a lake. Even fearing the cold mysterious water that swirls beneath the board, we still take the breath and plunge into the freedom of the unknown. The world may disappear, but the illusion of security that the shore offers is not important. What matters is our commitment to the Encounter--to Life. In a time of spiritual testing, we are called to move beyond our fears. This is when we need to let down our walls and defenses and stretch ourselves to manifest our highest possibilities. We can only become fully alive as we develop the inner strength to live with sometimes almost overwhelming anxiety and insecurity, as well as the sensitivity required by our creative passion.

REVERSED

If the Wands *Hod* position is reversed, fear is stopping us from fulfilling our potential. A greater understanding of the dynamics of fear is needed. We may ask, "What is the worst that can happen if I do this?"

Really examine your worst imagining, then ask "what then?"

With each answer, keep asking this question as you enter into, visualize and examine the worst result.

Inaction is still action. Stagnation is not a solution.

This reversal reminds us that our situation now requires a commitment to stay in the dynamic present rather than reacting in a habitual way. If we submit to fear and doubt, we will freeze our potential and stifle our creative connection. Trusting, or at least acting as we might if we did have trust, is essential so that we may take a needed plunge into the chill dark water wherein our treasure lies.

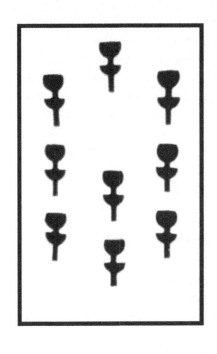 

9 YESOD OF WANDS

Essence: Preparation. Perspiration is required for our inspiration to manifest. Now we build the sweat equity essential to any lasting creative work. If you're a healer, chef, or musician, practice. If you're a writer, edit and rewrite. Even if the work is boring and frustrating, it is necessary.

The *Yesod (*nine) of Wands is the foundation of creation: work, the basis of manifestation. It is the ninety-percent-perspiration necessary to fully manifest the ten-percent-inspiration. Having had the faith and taken the leap into the unknown to follow our dream, we are now given courage to follow our vision. Knowing only our labor and sweat can make it happen, we may sometimes feel overwhelmed by the responsibilities and tasks that creativity requires. But self-discipline and perseverance is essential. Here, the musician practices six hours a day or more, so that the fingers are fast enough, strong enough, flexible enough, and knowledgeable enough to allow the essence, the heart, spirit, and soul of the music to pour through them into expression. So it must be with any creative endeavor.

REVERSED

When *Yesod* of Wands is reversed, either the work required is more difficult than we are capable of doing at this time or we are not working hard enough. Temptation to laziness and distraction can interfere with or prevent the completion of our work, or stunt our full expression.

It is essential to be aware that the work required often is not merely our involvement with the dynamics of completing physical tasks. It is also the work of accepting our responsibility for diligence, as we must develop our psychological and spiritual alertness to our internal processes and automatic/habitual responses.

We are reminded that sometimes it's easier to live in hell than to expand our awareness and allow ourselves the experience of heaven.

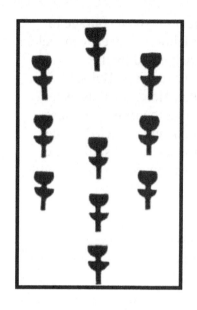 

10 MALKHUT OF WANDS

Essence: The full manifestation of inspiration and spiritual growth has been reached. That which once existed only in the realm of the ideal has become real. Contemplation and rest: this is a time for non-doing and profound openness.

The *Malkhut* of Wands refers to a time of *Shabbat*, of religious contemplation or meditation. We have breathed out, exhaling our life-work into the world. We now must allow inhalation to follow. This involves a time for non-doing, a profound openness, dwelling in the space between breaths until we are breathed into, *inspired*. We have been and experienced our selves as co-creators with The Eternal. We now can contemplate our creation and await our re-creation, next inspiration from Divine Source.

The *Malkhut* (ten) of Wands represents the highest potential of the Wands energies and the transitional or pivotal point, which unites Wands to the following Cups suit. In the ten of Wands, the work of manifestation is finished. The inspiration, work, practice and refinement of our creative imaginings are actualized in the world and the cycle of artistic inspiration and spiritual growth has reached the point of completion.

We are reminded that, rather than escapes, fascinations and the accumulation of stuff, it is love and joy, physical pleasure and the myriad offerings of the natural world that give the product of our inspiration meaning. Our deep heart-felt sense of gratitude guarantees our inspiration is not a trick or gimmick, but a true expression of connection. In the *Malkhut* of Wands we experience a time of goodness, allowing our emotions to flow. We know ourselves to be a child of the universe, a lover in the dance and dancer in the love-celebration of Infinite Creator and life.

REVERSED

When reversed the *Malkhut* of Wands card is a reminder that we are being too controlling and continuing to demand constant production from others or ourself. We need to release what has become a habit of pushing too hard. Take space to sit back, let go and rest in order to be renewed. This is not a time for control but rather a time for letting go, to allow life to flow through us, to simply happen.

In the act of breathing we can't only exhale or inhale. When we are in tune with our process, we allow ourselves time to contemplate what we have created. We are called upon to recognize and bless our creation pronouncing it good, in gratitude. Here, the *Malkhut* card's reversal reminds us that if we want to avoid burn-out we need to use this time for rest and renewal after having given birth to our latest creation.

QUEEN OF WANDS

Essence: A warm highly creative intuitive woman. She is inspiring, generous, a good friend: Possibly an artist. She can be fiery but not manipulative or underhanded.

The Queen of Wands represents one who is deeply connected with the Creative and yet grounded and rooted also in the world. Capable of joining both energies, the Queen looks back over her shoulder while her body faces forward. Her hand reaches palm up toward the flaming branch that floats beside her. Here the psychic manifests in her effortless creative generosity. Being one with the Energy that directs her life, there is no need to be manipulative. She can be kind, adaptable, a good, trustworthy friend, inspired and inspiring. She is an artist in whatever area she chooses, including those areas which are not commonly thought of as artistic; homemaking, teaching, mathematics, or science. Her particular occupation isn't important but rather the high degree of creativity she brings to all her endeavors elevates even the most mundane activities to an art. Because she fosters creativity in others, she can also be a good, understanding mentor or teacher.

The Queen of Wands does not pretend to be what she is not. She responds honestly when her opinion is sought. Full of energy, she is the muse amused; goodness, gracious, great leaves of fire. Since change is so much a part of creativity, she is adaptable, and may be unpredictable, but never petty or underhanded. She is warm and at times fiery.

REVERSED

When reversed, or in negative manifestation, the queen can seem hidden, unreachable or remote. She may be too lost or absorbed in her own world to attend to practical matters. Her personal relationships may suffer, as the requirements of her creative spirit and inspiration may absent her from those who seek her support while she follows her muse.

Also, the energy with which she expresses herself may make her appear to be impatient, domineering or too authoritarian. When uninspired she feels cut off from Source. This can make her unhappy, depressed and irritable. The best cure is for her to begin to produce something, anything. The very act, even if unsuccessful when viewed from a critical perspective, is necessary to unblock any stuck physical, emotional or spiritual energy and reawaken her vital connection.

KING OF WANDS

Essence: Creative and spiritual, he's a dreamer. A truly independent spirit, he can be a good husband, but his freedom is paramount. Being receptive, empathic and playful, the King is able to inspire the young and can be good father, teacher and partner.

The King of Wands is a man who, like the Queen, is connected with the creative. The flaming wand grows up beside him. King of the Wood, he is the King of green branches in the warmth of the sun, one with the creative abundance of the summer, laughing and playful. The king is a truly independent spirit whose freedom comes from his connection to Source. He has an enormous capacity for creative work. He is one whose masculine energy manifests as a dreamer who can channel the animating fire, represented by his salamander, that unites all life in the co-creating. This is a man who can be sympathetic and even motherly, for he is so receptive to the Feminine aspect. He is trustworthy, and honest, a good friend and father. His male and female aspects are welded into one, so her understands, teaches, sympathizes with, and inspires the young. The King of Wands is never mean, petty or manipulative. He is proud but not usually prideful. He is a magician, although not necessarily the kind that does tricks. His magic is the artistic manifestation of his creative channeling. He may be a religious leader or a spiritual person.

REVERSED

When the card is reversed, it may indicate insensitivity to the feelings of others. Because he can become so involved in his creative endeavors, he can shut out his own physical needs as well as the physical or emotional needs of others. He can be impractical, someone with his head in the clouds. He can be unpredictable but never boring. Since money is not of any particular importance, he may or may not have very much, although there's usually enough to get by.

As a potential partner it's important to know he views financial security or any other security as illusory. This belief, which can appear as stinginess, may make him insecure about resources. Or he may seem reluctant to make a concrete commitment, since in his philosophy, change is the only thing he knows can be counted on.

PRINCESS OF WANDS

Essence: Intuitive wisdom and a sympathetic nature makes this sensitive, artistic, often young female or male person a dreamer or visionary. This being may be corporeal or appear as a dream messenger or spiritual guide.

The Princess of Wands is a beautiful young woman or girl. She's a dreamer and can be a clear channel for spiritual energies, a muse, or messenger. She can come from our dreams, or lead us back to them. The Princess of Wands may also refer to an inquisitive young man or boy who has these traits of sensitive receptivity to the music of the spheres and to the gifts of the creative force of inspiration.

The Princess can be inventive, dramatic and whimsical. With a somewhat otherworldly look, she rests, sitting a little in front of or under a tree. The dark flame-like branches bend to merge with her crown, while the light of her inner self flames up into the tree. Her appearance is almost medieval, indicating that she is not only of this time. She is connected to ancient energies and to the fluidity of youth. The tree is not only plant-like, but also has an almost human shape. This indicates the mutability of the dream wherein she dwells. She may be musical or artistic: a gift giver, although the gift may be spiritual rather than material. The Princess card may even represent the gift. Depending on the surrounding cards, it might indicate the arrival of good news or a spiritual healing. She is usually telepathic and helpful, and the news she carries may be the same.

The gift offered by the Princess of Wands can also appear in a dream. Dreams not only give us valuable insights about our everyday life, they can also be clairvoyant or telepathic.

Visionaries from all cultures have accorded the highest respect to dreams and other manifestations of the unconscious. Dreams can also be a direct communication from Spirit.

REVERSED

When reversed, the Princess of Wands card indicates one who is so engaged in day dreams that they are not able to function at their full capacity in world. If this is the case it indicates a need to return to earth. Dreams can only manifest or be of use to us if we remain grounded in life. Other wise they're just smoke-dreams.

This reversal may even indicate someone who is literally (because of drugs) or figuratively living in a trance. If this is the case, it's a message telling us it's time to wake up and smell the coffee. Dreams and fantasies must be subjected to the clear light of day for their true value to be known.

PRINCE OF WANDS

Essence: A child or childishly impulsive, impatient person who needs to develop receptivity and trust to realize their creative potential. Or it may indicate a serendipitous message or discovery.

The Prince of Wands may announce the arrival of an inspiring or fortunate message. When referring to a person, the Prince of Wands is a scholar: friendly, inquisitive and possibly creative, his impulsiveness, spiritual impatience and his scholarliness keep him off center. In the realm of creativity we need to be receptive rather than pursuant.

It may indicate one who is caught in the impatient acquisitiveness of youth, or it may represent a young person (male or female) who has not yet matured. In this card, his hand is still partially outstretched toward the figure before him. As in the myth of Apollo and Daphne, in chasing and attempting to possess or force Inspiration from Creative Source, he has inadvertently caused it to fly from him. The tree before him has the figure of a woman caught in the action of running from his spiritually acquisitive energy and need to control what is essentially Holy Great Spirit's bestowal or revelation.

Here his feminine side has not yet been integrated into his consciousness, and therefore he has cut himself off from what he most fervently desires. His mouth is still open from talking rather than listening.

There is hope that this may not be a permanent situation. The branch above his head is still awaiting his notice and attention, if he can stop his overly intellectual approach and tune into his unconscious. He's called upon to trust the creative energy to be there. Instead of attempting to force it, he can cultivate a little emptiness. Then, the Creative will have room to enter.

REVERSED

If the card is reversed, it refers to one who is an energy drain on others, through talking and never listening. It might be indicating someone who has a pompous, overly intellectual approach to life.

This card could also refer to a woman or man who acts too much from the energy of animus, reflecting the androcentric, patriarchal values of our contemporary culture, and who thus freezes his or her own creativity.

KETAR, ACE OF CUPS

Essence: *Ketar* of Cups embraces the essence and potential of the Cups suit: the watery realm which dissolves boundaries, governs our emotions and capacity for love and relationship. It is about values--what we value and how our relationships evolve, reflect and express our values.

The *Ketar* of Cups represents the realm of feeling—emotion and the capacity for love and relationship. It is the gift that gives and receives. It is the transcendent Love that is the breath of life. Where the *Ketar,* Ace of Wands is the inspiration to create, the Ace of Cups is the motivation.

Ketar of Cups reflects the central mother, *Mem*, embracing the element Water. In the pictorial image, the waters above and the waters below eternally fill and pour forth from the cup. It is our capacity for feeling. In the sphere of emotion, the realm of valuing is where we decide what we believe is good or bad. It is the beginning of love, joy, abundance, healing power and fecundity.

It is the ability to merge, to change and be changed by what we love, for *Ketar* of Cups contains the mutable water of love that destroys egotism. Through recognizing and valuing the other, as we also would wish to be seen and valued, we close the gulf that separates us from others and our world. The *Ketar* of Cups is about our ability to love, to touch and to be touched, including but not limited to the transcendent power of sex.

In the Ace of Cups peace, reciprocity, the union of soul mates, infinite compassion, spiritual sustenance, and the path of the heart are initiated.

REVERSED

When the *Ketar* of Cups is reversed it represents emotional repression or denial concerning emotions or feelings. It is an indication that we are confused about our feelings and emotions. Or, it might be an indication that although we think we are making clear choices unclouded by emotion, actually the reverse is true. We may be emotionally cut off and removed rather than engaged.

When we deny rather than face our negative emotions, we give them more power to cause harm. The choice is always ours. By admitting our shadow into consciousness, painful though it is to our egos, we become free and able to receive the blessings of love, connection, relationship, and emotional growth contained in the upright *Ketar* of Cups

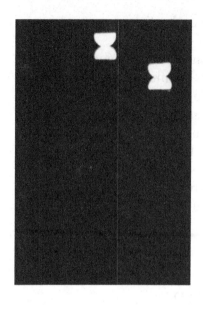
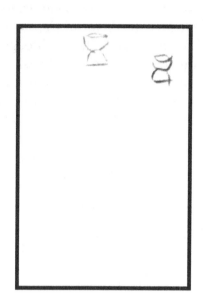

2 HOKHMA OF CUPS

Essence: Ready for relationship, openness and anticipation. Feeling comfortable and happy alone awakens the desire to share ourselves with a mate, partner or others with whom we can build a deep relationship.

   The *Hokhma* (two) of Cups represents the realization of our desire to find a mate, collaborator or work-partner. We are comfortable in our skin, sensing our own individuality. Even when alone, we enjoy our life and creativity, while simultaneously yearning to share our love, creativity and life with another. We are whole, integrated and also open for another to enter. There is a readiness for relationship.

No longer fearing a lonely future, we know how to create our own joy and life. The cup of our heart is no longer filled to overflowing with yearning. We don't need another to make us happy and so our heart, emptied of longing, has room for love to pour in and fill it.

We may experience feelings of anticipation and a sense of expectation awaiting an impending arrival. While knowing we can be happy alone, we are nevertheless available to love and intimate relationships.

REVERSED

When the *Hokhma* of Cups is reversed, we feel lonely and incomplete without a mate. We may believe our only possibility for joy and happiness in life depends on our finding someone to love and be loved by. This may leave us so intensely filled with longing for a friend, a mate, or a child, that nothing can enter. The ground is too full of bitterness, fear or grief. It is important at this time to find happiness within our selves.

We are being invited to release our fear of being alone and seek our awareness of connection first within our own heart. Now is not the time to look for someone to love us or make us happy. With no beloved other in our life, we need to accept that we can't count on an ephemeral future. The present is all we have.

What is not here will not be out there. The only future we can count on is our life as it is now. Ask, "If I'm to be alone forever, do I choose to be happy alone or unhappy alone?" If we choose to be happy alone, we may find this choice is the very thing that empties our cup of longing so that love can fill it.

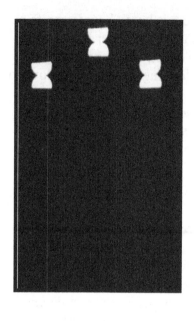
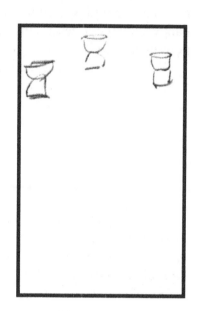

3 BINAH OF CUPS

Essence: The process of falling in love, or reawakening our love again for the world, our life, our purpose, a beloved, or a friend. Euphoria, joy and a sense of discovery fills our heart. This is an exciting magical time of closeness, shared growth and gratitude.

The *Binah* (three) of Cups contains the process of falling in love. It energizes all aspects of our life bringing forth feelings of intense euphoria, joy, and harmony. We share our dreams and life stories. There is a feeling of having discovered a place where we can express our whole selves, someone we can really talk to. We experience an intense drive to be fused with the object of our love. Now that we have finally discovered our perfect place or soul mate, even the most mundane things, when done together, take on a magical and wondrous quality. This is a time of sharing growth on many levels, of deep communication and communion.

Although by necessity this heightened state is temporary, it nevertheless can form the foundation for dedication to our life's true passion, and to love and a lasting relationship.

It often involves the discovery of the anima or animus in the other. Those repressed, neglected or latent qualities, which we may not yet but need to see in our selves, are enlivened and revealed. This is a wonderful time for learning and expanding awareness of our potential.

The *Binah* of Cups may also represent a time in an established relationship when both parties suddenly look at each other with new eyes, and their appreciation and love's original intensity is rekindled. It is these moments that nourish even longstanding relationships. It may be that after a time of taking them for granted, we are awakened again to the value and importance of our longstanding friendships.

This might simply describe our awakening to those moments that nourish and enlighten any aspect of our life and life's work. The passion and dedication we feel for our chosen path, although not romantic, can also be imbued with the transformative magic which makes it as necessary, vital and important as a personal relationship.

REVERSED

When reversed, this card may indicate a one-sided or imbalanced love where one person loves more than the other. Or it might indicate unrequited love.

It could be a signal or caution that, just as a student who believes her teacher, when he looks toward her side of the room, is making eyes just at her, we are indulging in a one-sided or delusional projection.

The *Binah* reversed can serve as a warning against the delusional belief that we can make or force the object of our desire to fall in love with us. Such delusions create a dangerous, or at the very least an unfulfilling situation.

When we examine our projections and reclaim them as our own we learn much from this experience. In reclaiming our projections and realizing that the beauty and gifts we see in the other are actually our own, we free ourselves and take back our power.

4 HESED OF CUPS

Essence: Our absorption in the other has led to self-abandonment. In all relationships, the act of falling in love lands us eventually in reality. We are called upon to wake up and open our eyes.

The *Hesed* of Cups is the card of marriage. Our life has finally become committed or joined with the beloved. The individual lives of the lovers are now fused into one. No longer walking a cloud, we now find ourselves suddenly dropping back down to earth, to reality.

Or perhaps, if we have finally birthed a beautiful anticipated child, project or other
co-creation, we suddenly feel we have no life, since our life has been totally absorbed by our offspring's needs.

Once we and our beloved possess each other, it's easy to feel we own each other. The danger is that we lose the awareness that we are separate individuals. This of course can be applied to any business partnership or shared artistic endeavor.

The true emotional, physical and energetic cost of the project or relationship begins to make itself known. Day in and day out, we discover we not only have married each other, but each other's families, friends, tastes, parenting styles, personal ambitions, and bad habits. Even where there is true love and great happiness, the waters are never unruffled, the sailing never completely smooth. Even in the most successful marriages, when we look back over the shared years of life together, the best we can hope for is that our life has been mostly filled with love, and mostly happy ever after.

Although this card appears to be the opposite of what we would like, it is actually an opportunity for growth, self-discovery, true knowing of another, and the extraordinary experience of true love without any illusions.

REVERSED

When the *Hesed* of Cups is reversed, it may indicate we are dangerously imbalanced. Our ego has become overly identified with and totally submerged in the beloved. In the expansive oneness of the *Hesed* reversed we suddenly find we have lost our selves. We don't really want to be someone's right arm or better half. We are becoming too absorbed by the values, ideas and needs of others. Our shared life has become habituated and routine. We may be feeling bored or trapped.

We need to ask ourselves "What am I not communicating?"

"Am I not expressing my needs out of a need to keep peace, or out of fear?"

"What am I afraid of seeing?"

"What truth am I hiding?"

"Why can't I allow my authentic self to be seen?"

This reversal may also be an indication of emotional enslavement or martyrdom.

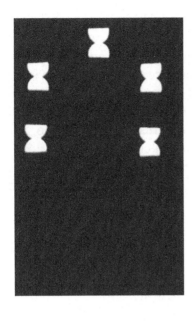 

5 GEVURAH OF CUPS

Essence: We come back to our selves. The challenge or demands of the project or relationship become clear. We realize we are still individuals. Our own needs and sense of self forces us to emerge from absorption in the relationship's cocoon and grow.

The *Gevurah* (five) of Cups refers to a time of emotional contraction. Having given ourselves away, we now take ourselves back. Suddenly we find ourselves in the opposite position from our *Binah,* longing for togetherness. Now our desire is to contract and assert our separateness. We no longer want to be absorbed in another and look instead at our differences. It may be that the very thing we loved in the other shows its annoying side. The free spirit we married seems irresponsible. That responsible and prudent person is suddenly seen as uptight and overly controlled or controlling.

Where in the *Hesed* of Cups we said, "I love you completely; take all of me; I want to satisfy your every need," we now say, "Prove you love me; I also have needs; give me some space."

In the *Gevurah* of Cups we experience the karma of having been taken for granted, or of ourself taking the beloved for granted. Stereotypical and habitual ways of seeing and relating to each other becomes a source of growing discomfort. We no longer see one another as we are, but feel confined in our beloved's stagnant vision. Unless we recognize each other's continually evolving selves, we risk the relationship exploding in our faces.

The *Gevurah* of Cups looks like a rocket or firecracker, and so it is. If used well, this explosive energy can light up the dark sky of illusion and by its light reveal new areas for communication, growth and awareness.

This is a time of struggle between polarities. Because we have contracted to take back ourselves, we are now suddenly offered the opportunity to see each other more clearly.

REVERSED

When the *Gevurah* of Cups is reversed, it may point to a time when the truth of who the individuals in the relationship really are, is revealed. In the light, all we have kept secret or hidden shows itself. This may be too difficult for the relationship to bear.

An extreme example might be that our mate who had been easily jealous and controlling suddenly turns scary or abusive. An overly solicitous mate suddenly reveals that they never loved us, or has found someone new and are now leaving. Or, we discover our partner has a hidden and therefore unrecognized addiction.

At any rate, the reversed Gevurah of Cups can indicate a severe lack of communication. This may either spell the end of the relationship or a huge opportunity for growth and healing. When the masks come off, we can learn to really love.

172

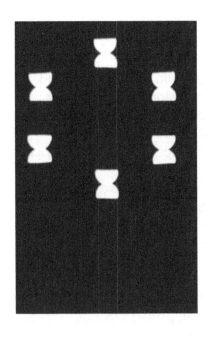 

6 TIFERET OF CUPS

Essence: Personal growth within the relationship. We learn to balance our absorption in and nurturing of a relationship with our need to withdraw. Still committed to the relationship, we take ourselves back to nurture our own needs, desires and interests as well.

The *Tiferet* (six) of Cups represents compassion, empathy, true understanding. The soul-mates are joined, but in a vital relationship where both the dark and light sides of the partners are revealed to each other and themselves.

Though it is not without conflict, it is a dance where the partners have their differences and yet accept themselves and each other. Snow White turns out to be a lousy housekeeper without her retinue of dwarves. Prince Charming never picks up his clothes or puts the toilet seat down. She likes parties and travel while he needs quiet and time to be alone. Yet their love allows each to fully grow and be themselves. They share a love deeper than each their differences and flaws.

The *Tiferet* of Cups combines passion for each other and self-love. Communication and compassion are joined. Both parties are committed and dedicated to keeping the relationship true, vital and alive. Their recognition and respect for their differences and different needs, increases their love and enriches them both.

The *Tiferet* of Cups represents a time when we may look at our mutual creation that is a relationship and appreciate its goodness.

This card refers to a way of being in all our relationships. The relationship with a beloved is only used as an example, since the *Tiferet* of Cups can refer to any or all of our important relationships. In an individual reading it may refer to the relationship between parent and child, between friends, or even a business partnership.

REVERSED

When the *Tiferet* of Cups is reversed, it is a reminder that life can always cause even the most secure and established relationships to change course. It addresses the importance of staying current in our awareness of each other. *Tiferet* reversed may be trying to warn us against becoming complacent.

We need to ask ourselves "Am I seeing my partner as they truly are or am I projecting onto them my own reality?"

"Am I really willing to listen to what they are trying to communicate?"

"Am I willing to ask a hard question?"

"Can I speak my truth?"

Conflict is important for growth. If we only see our own distorted projection of our partner, even if it's an attractive picture, we put our selves and our relationship in danger. All that can help is vigilance so that we can see through the projections to the reality.

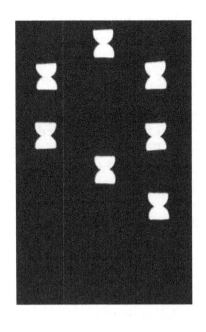
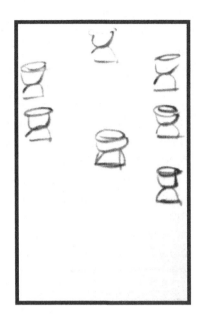

7 NETZACH OF CUPS

Essence: Relaxation and joy born of mutual fulfillment as the relationship grows effortlessly. This is a restful, contemplative period, a time of internal growth, like an untroubled pregnancy (either figurative or literal).

The *Netzach* (seven) of Cups represents a time of deep mutual fulfillment for the relationship. The relationship grows without apparent effort on our part. It is a time of relaxation and joy. It is, for example, the restful contemplation and unhurried pace of an easy pregnancy. This card represents the internal growth necessary before the relationship can expand into the world in a new way or with a new orientation. As partners we review our shared past, grateful for the mutual efforts that have brought us to this present moment.

As we may also be partner to our self, we may have recently

resolved an internal conflict. Now, no longer divided into two minds or hearts in a matter, the partner this card refers to may actually be an aspect of our own internal self.

When we are at rest, we have a chance to re-collect ourselves and gather strength as we look forward to a new beginning. This may take the form of a physical child, or any other new shared endeavor or labor of love that will expand from the protected womb of our relationship into the world. Possibly our priorities have shifted in an unexpected direction that requires us to use this break in momentum to prepare for the beginning of a renewed expansiveness.

Growth now involves an internal, possibly unconscious or undirected process. What is needed is patience, appreciation, mutual nurturing of each other and creative openness. There is no need to push the river. Instead we are called upon to allow ourselves to drift on the current and absorb the beauty that surrounds us. A time to enjoy, be grateful, and just be.

REVERSED

The *Netzach* of Cups reversed may be an indication that we are coveting the good fortune of others instead of appreciating and cultivating our own relationship. We may feel like an outsider and resent other people for blessings that appear to come so easily to them while they are so hard for us to attain.

The reversal of the *Netzah* can indicate the need to take responsibility for the difficulties or shortcomings we are experiencing as we try to create and maintain healthy, fulfilling relationships. Only then can we find the resources and develop the skills we need to create the kinds of relationships we aspire to.

This reversal may occasionally signal an unrealistic or inappropriate yearning for a child, as in the case of a couple who wants a child to keep their marriage together, or the woman or teenager who wishes for a baby to have somebody to love them.

Finally, this reversal might refer to the desire to jump into a marriage or partnership prematurely, without really understanding what such a partnership would involve.

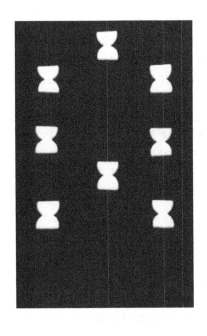
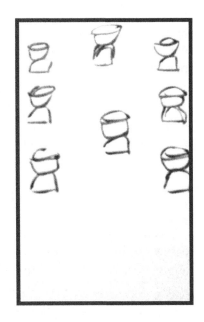

8 HOD OF CUPS

Essence: Following rest and reflection, we welcome the new elements introduced into our relationship, though we again must face unexpected demands, stresses and frustrations that push us to grow and adapt to new challenges.

The *Hod* (eight) of Cups represents the reverberation from the idyll of the *Netzach* (seven) of Cups. The child has been born. The parents or partners discover that the mutual nurturing of the product of their relationship is its own product and demands work.

The stress of parenthood, the unexpected differences in parenting styles and values, differing emotional and/or physical energy levels: all of these put new and more complex demands on the partners. There is a call for increased communication, compromise, emotional and physical commitment.

This is a time of conflict and even rage we never thought we had, a time of growth as we again struggle to learn how to resolve differences and preserve our self as well as our relationship. This can be difficult and often frustrating. As we are pushed beyond what we thought were our limits we discover capacities for love, understanding, compassion and a level of patience and forgiveness we never imagined we had.

The *Hod* of Cups also pertains to the struggles any effective group goes through. It reflects the necessary, and often painful lessons we must absorb as we learn to handle our emotional responsibilities to the group.

REVERSED

When the *Hod* of Cups is reversed, we may be attempting to escape from conflict or avoid communication by internalizing anger, sorrow, disappointment or frustration. It may be that some of the feelings we are experiencing seem somehow unacceptable or go against the image we like to have of ourselves. We try not to see them. It is important to realize that ignoring feelings does not make them go away.

We must ask ourselves, "What am I trying to hide from myself?"

"What am I afraid of seeing?"

"Why am I afraid to communicate with my partner?"

If this state of withheld communication continues, it can be damaging to us as well as to any of our relationships.

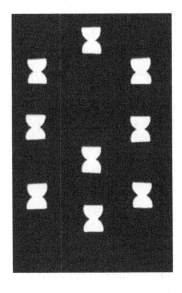 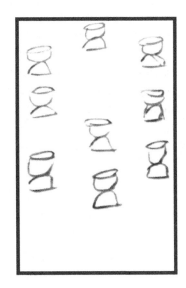

9 YESOD OF CUPS

Essence: We enter the ongoing process of self-knowing and of letting ourselves be known by others. We continue to discover how to live with our own and another's imperfections, while we increase our ability to cultivate and nurture our authentic selves.

The *Yesod* (nine) of Cups represents how we are able to link ourselves to the whole. It is the foundation of all true and fruitful relationships, the ongoing process of self-knowing and allowing our self to be known. We learn to live honestly with our own and others' imperfections and vulnerability. We engage in the process of questioning and awareness. Our capacity for seeing the truth of who we are, and for staying in touch with that dynamic truth, becomes the foundation for all our relationships. The ability to combine truthfulness and compassion determines our relationship's vitality and degree of mutual satisfaction and learning.

How responsible and committed we are to following our heart's wisdom will determine where that path will lead. We learn that relationship is not some thing done to us or for us, but like a garden takes constant nurturing and care. We develop the skills to recognize our destructive patterns, weeding out false judgments, cultural expectations, past injuries and our own insecurities. If we want beautiful flowers and fruits, we must pool our energies and work together.

REVERSED

When the *Yesod* of Cups is reversed, it means we are taking too much for granted. It is a reminder that we need to take more responsibility for our relationships and not expect a garden that is uncared for to feed us. We are called upon to work on uprooting the weeds beneath which our flowers struggle.

The reversed *Yesod* calls us to become more conscious. To be unconscious is to be out of touch. If we lose our capacity for seeing the truth and staying in touch with each other, either literally or figuratively, we damage the foundation of our relationships. This leads to self-deception and to our being the subject of deception.

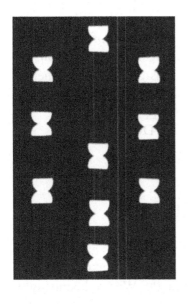 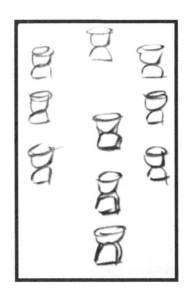

10 MALKHUT OF CUPS

Essence: Love brings the heart's repose. Perfection is experienced as an ever-changing experience of Love's manifestation in a long-term relationship, both mundane and miraculous.

The *Malkhut* (ten) of Cups is the earth, the material world where we can actually touch God in our relationships. Here, love in all its totality brings the heart's repose. Perfection is experienced as an ever-changing experience of love's manifestations. We have entered the essential Holy wholeness. The highest and most profound is united with the lowest and most mundane of our activities. Even when we are deep in the well, beneath the dark waters of conflict, anger and frustration, we feel the shining fluorescence--the enlightening Light, Love.

All of experience is permeated with the manifestation of the Divine when we take responsibility for our contact with the deep inner source, which is always whole and perfect.

There is Grace even in our most mundane actions: organizing a space or project, cleaning up a mess, housework, child-care, correcting punctuation. The conscious realization of our participation in the miraculous now manifests in our relationship to life. This card represents a depth and history of commitment and responsibility that many years of shared love and compassion have forged. We are grateful for blessings. Our Prayers and efforts flow together with the Divine.

REVERSED

When the *Malkhut* of Cups is reversed, there is an inability to see the forest for the trees. Confusion or lack of perspective due to old or habitual ways of relating dominate. We are losing sight of the whole as we become consumed with petty disagreements and difficulties. Things of no real significance are getting blown out of proportion. Let them go. If you get tired of picking up your partner's socks off the living room floor, learn to live with a messy house or hire a housekeeper. Or, choose to live separately even while still in love. Explore what options are possible if we allow ourselves to think outside the box.

The reversal of the *Malkhut* may indicate a time when we need to ask ourselves, "What in this relationship, or in my expectations, do I need to alter or let go?"

Finally, as the *Malkhut* position in any suit is symbolic of a culmination, this card is about the part of loving that involves letting go. It can mean letting go of fruitless expectations that people's natures will change. It can refer to the letting go of children so that they can make their own lives. It may involve letting go of each other, as we all must in the end.

When we release our grasp on the other and let go, only the clinging is gone. Love alone remains.

QUEEN OF CUPS

Essence: One whose life is permeated with spiritual and emotional connectedness. She is empathic, compassionate, flexible, nurturing and devoted in her intimate relationships. Expressive of the Holy Feminine, she is egalitarian, affectionate, sensuous and sexual.

The Queen of Cups is a self-directed, non-authoritarian, religious or spiritual woman. Being one whose life is permeated with an awareness of her relationship to the people and the life energy around her. She imbues all with her sense of spiritual connection to the Whole. She is the archetypal female and as such may be a mother, priestess or possibly an artist, poet or musician. Wherever her creative energy is engaged she expresses and reflects her emotional connectedness. At her best, she is intuitively capable of giving to each what they need; food, affection, laughter, spiritual comfort, or compassion. Open-hearted and generous, she can be imaginative and romantic, and also a devoted mother, whether or not she has children. A lover of life, she is responsive to the needs of those around her.

Because of her sensual connection to the natural world, the Queen is sensitive to the constantly changing flow of her own energy cycles, physical needs, and her connection to the Mother of All. With the merging and blending properties of water she is acutely sensitive and aware of the relationships between things, even those which appear to be unrelated.

The emblems of this archetype are the moon, the gentle dove and the transformative serpent. She wears the serpent on her head like the priestesses of the Great Mother. A cup surrounded by the triple moon appears behind and above her, representing the many trinitarian aspects of creation: blood, milk and water; life, death and rebirth; fire, water and air; youth, maturity and age. All are the Goddess's domain.

Unlike the creativity of the Queen of Wands, the Queen of Cup's creativity is the realm of emotion, love and relationship. She is a sexual and sensuous person.

REVERSED

Like the water element to which the Queen is connected, she can be unpredictable and moody. She can change, sometimes in a flash, from equanimity to wrath; or from a thunderstorm of temper to joyous laughter to the calm of a placid lake.

When reversed, her archetype may represent an overly temperamental woman given to self-dramatization or irrationality. She can be a raw nerve. Relationships can become problematic and difficult to maintain due to a tendency to manifest the more destructive emotions.

The important thing to remember in this reversal, is whatever feeling she's manifesting is subject to change in a relatively short time. Although her highest energy is love, it may be immature or narcissistic, in which case there is a need to learn and develop emotional restraint and compassion for herself and others.

The Queen of Cups reversed may also simply indicate that the person manifesting the qualities of the archetype (of the upright or reversed card position) is male rather than female.

KING OF CUPS

Essence: A wise, kind, mature man comfortable in the emotional realm. He is a good father, counselor or teacher who views change philosophically. He sees transformation and change as a necessary manifestation of the order in chaos.

The King of Cups represents a wise older man. He is full of love and kindness prompted by his ability to feel deeply and empathetically. His being twinkles like sunlight on water. The dove of the Goddess is in his heart. The dolphin dances in his hand and the moon's phases float like bubbles in and out of his cup-shaped crown. He is immersed in the sensitive chaos of life. Emotions are under his control so he's not swept away with their tides. Being a good husband and father, he behaves toward others in a warm and supportive way. A good advisor and counselor, with a loving and nurturing manner in his relationships, the King represents a *mensch* (fully responsible ethical human being).

The archetype embodied in The King of Cups expresses the manifestation of the loving Father God and his creative life of compassionate, sustaining energy. This is the masculine counterpart of the Queen of Cups. Like her, he also is a sensuous and sexual being.

Where The Queen is the constancy and the unity at the hub of the changing emotional seasons, The King is the alert compassionate observer who evaluates and helps each find its rightful place in the whole.

REVERSED

When the King of Cups is reversed, it may indicate one who is too moody or lacking adequate emotional control. Like the Queen in reversed position, he may be a dangerous narcissist using his empathic awareness of other's emotions to manipulate them for his own ends. Or, this card may indicate one who is emotionally immature, over-sensitive, possibly an alcoholic or addict. Either way, it indicates one who can drag others down with his moods or withdraw into his own depths, becoming unreachable until his inner storms clear.

Buffeted about by acute sensitivity, he can be over-protective of self or others. He can be vengeful, arrogant and conceited. In either case it is the result of the mistaken attempt to control forces that by their nature need freedom to flourish and grow.

The King of Cups reversed may also simply indicate that the person manifesting the qualities of the archetype (of the upright or reversed card position) is female rather than male.

PRINCESS OF CUPS

Essence: The new moon. A usually feminine archetype of a joyful, curious, romantic person. One who is affectionate and open hearted, youthful, loving and lovable. Although moody the moods don't usually last long. When not referring to an actual person she represents our need to express and share love, heartfelt joy, playfulness and enjoyment of life and the pleasures of the sensual world.

Beneath her crescent crown is the warm and slightly mischievous smile of a younger sister who offers a cup of sparkling wine, balanced delicately and effortlessly between her fingers. This archetype encompasses the romantic, playful, curious nature and innocent vulnerability of youth.

When the Princess appears in our life the energy she represents is that of a bubbly, affectionate, open-hearted, generous and inviting person--loving and lovable. Her vitality, like a clear stream, reveals the shimmering depths of her soul. This has given her an optimistic and trusting nature. Generosity of spirit and wholeheartedness bring support for all endeavors. She is open about her feelings, and trustworthy. Usually cheerful, her angry or melancholy moods rarely last. She is beloved, sensuous and delighted by life.

When someone is reflecting this archetype they're one whose life has been like a brook traversing a countryside filled with fields and wildflowers, woods and gentle hills. We may find the depths of innate wisdom and creativity are benefited when we join together with inspiring friends, where the learning and teaching are reciprocal, or by seeking the guidance of a wise guide or teacher who, like a riverbed, can hold and guide our energy.

The Princess card when not referring to an actual person can represent the new moon, awakening of love, our need to express and share love, heartfelt joy, playfulness and enjoyment of life and the pleasures of the sensual world.

REVERSED

When reversed, The Princess can be easily distracted or careless. Especially when she is swept up with enthusiastic enjoyment she may lose sight of the ground and her footing.

There is some danger that our energy will slowly dissipate into selfish complacency and emotional immaturity. This may be a warning concerning a tendency to stagnate.

This archetype may also indicate a shallow and self-indulgent young person or woman who uses her feminine wiles to manipulate others in order to further her own ends and ambitions. It may be a woman or a girl who uses the appearance of innocence to her own advantage. Finally, both this card and the Prince of Cups can represent our internal anima or animus, and the necessity of bringing these spontaneous internal manifestations of the self into the light of consciousness. They may operate in their most creative aspects, rather than their most destructive.

PRINCE OF CUPS

Essence: A masculine archetype of a romantic, humorous and charming youth, who is handsome, poetic, understanding and sensitive. This card may also refer to the arrival of a message of an emotional nature.

The Prince of Cups can symbolize communication concerning a love relationship. It might also indicate the search for a passion or that this is a time of emotional growth and experimentation. Allowing ourselves to risk some emotional vulnerability is necessary for growth. It may be time to follow our heart, rather than head, to trust in the absolutely irrational power of love.

The archetype of the Prince of Cups can represent a romantic young man: handsome, poetic, understanding and sensitive. He is a humorous and charming person. The soft dove-shaped beret he wears connects him to the Mother. With a seductive smile he offers a cup of sparkling wine to the person he desires. It is through offering himself that he finds the support he needs.

The ability to give himself wholeheartedly to any endeavor is his greatest strength and virtue. He can be a considerate and tender lover, brave and protective of his home and family. Like a rushing springtime river, his energy propels him, carrying others along with his intuitive leadership and enthusiastic momentum. It is therefore most important for this youth to remember to remain considerate of others. Even in his exuberance he must be careful not to lose touch with ethical values in the pursuit of his goals.

REVERSED

If the card is reversed, it may indicate a danger of throwing ourselves away or wasting energy on unworthy pursuits or people. It may be a warning against our selfish impulses and behavior or that of a friend or lover.

Reversed, the Prince may be hypocritical, giving only the appearance of positive aspects. Actually he is a seducer in the worst sense, for his own ends or ego.

He may need to develop circumspection and patience so that he does not throw himself away on unworthy people or pursuits. He may be manipulative of the emotions of others, a dance-away lover, full of hollow promises, irresponsible in his emotional treatment of others. Thus, this card reversed may indicate a need to wait and look carefully before being swept away by another's enthusiastic energy.

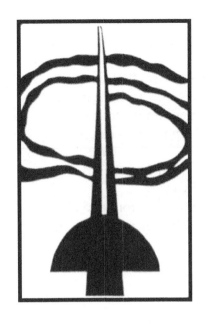
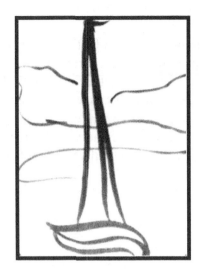

KETAR, ACE OF SWORDS

Essence: The thinking realm where we concentrate, evaluate and step back from our emotional investment and values to gain a more objective view. It concerns fairness, self-discipline, self-control, free will and our responsibility for the choices we make.

The *Ketar* (Ace) of Swords represents the capacity for thought, reasoning and observing how things work. It is our ability to use intellectual powers for understanding the world, for learning and study, either in school or independently.

We can step back from a situation we have been emotionally embroiled in and obtain a more objective view. Using the sword of reason we can cut to the underlying root of a situation.

Self-discipline and self-control enable us to concentrate and focus our mental energies to attain our goals. The *Ketar* of Swords expresses the potential for all mental powers and effects. Because the Sword cuts two ways, it represents duality and our power to choose. We can choose wisely between two competing perspectives. Thus, the *Ketar* of Swords represents the ability for equilibrium, for the skill to choose between opposites, to make balanced judgments and the scales of justice. It also represents the metaphoric or literal power of the surgeon who can cut away a gangrenous infection or perform a necessary caesarean, bringing a child forth who would otherwise die in utero.

The Bible story of King Solomon's wisdom when discerning which of two women claimants was the true mother of an infant is a perfect example of the *Ketar* of Swords.

Our focus and will can have great energy for good or evil. We are now held accountable for the choices we make.

REVERSED

When the *Ketar* of Swords is reversed, it may indicate an approach of aggression or a tendency to violence. We may be the subject of some injustice or treachery. Conversely, we may be tempted to act unjustly.

It can be an indication that we're being judgmental or unjust, or that our thinking is unbalanced or lacking in clarity. Possibly we are projecting our emotional baggage on a situation and need to step back, evaluate the root of our thinking and gain a more fair and balanced perspective. In the case of a potential surgery or resolution of a personal conflict, this position can be understood as a recommendation to get a second opinion.

Also, the reversed *Ketar* of Swords is an indication we've become so caught up in our process of gathering information about a subject, that we're held back from taking necessary action. We're trying to cut up reality into so many diverse parts that we become fragmented and hopelessly confused. We may be over-thinking a matter or situation.

When reversed, The *Ketar* may be signaling we need to examine more closely what we are creating since it can have unpredictable, unintended, unwanted and possibly disastrous consequences. Many scientific achievements have in themselves no moral or ethical compass: the discovery of nuclear fission, artificial intelligence, and gene splicing have opened doors to great good or destructive potential.

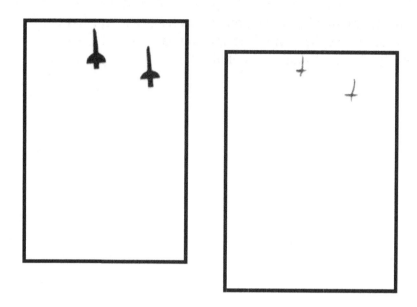

2 HOKHMAH OF SWORDS

Essence: Clearly seeing both sides of an issue. We weigh options and evaluate information. If required, we can fairly decide between opposing viewpoints or negotiate a middle way. This confers ability to discuss, communicate dispassionately, and prioritize. Gain or retain objectivity.

The *Hokhmah* (two) of Swords implies reasoning ability, comprehension and mechanical or intellectual brilliance, the capacity to see all sides of an issue. We have a need and natural ability to balance and weigh information. We can step outside ourselves to gain greater objectivity even if doing so may threaten our ego or self-interests. Meticulousness in this regard results in our clear evaluations of situations. This provides us with an unprejudiced and clear way of seeing and evaluating information, people and even our own behavior. We are open to constructive criticism and so are able to grow and make important changes in our life and relationships.

Often the Two of Swords expresses a need for self-expression through writing or discussion. It also indicates the use of these skills for settling conflicts, either within our own mind or in our relationships. There is increased understanding of opposing views, and an increased ability to negotiate, prioritize, and compromise. We can communicate our own views and also express an accurate comprehension of our opposition's views. This is a good time to settle a debate or resolve even a deep antagonism, creating a truce, or ending a conflict.

The *Hokhmah* of Swords may also suggest that since we are of two minds concerning a given matter it will be wise to take more time for evaluating or gathering the necessary information before making a decision.

REVERSED

When the *Hokhmah* of Swords is reversed, we are being warned this is not the time for indecision. If we wait too long, all may be lost.

This may also appear to remind us that it's important to remain flexible, and alert to a change in the wind. It is much easier to rescue our lawn furniture before the hurricane strikes than to have to carry it in against the gale.

Contrary Two of Swords can also indicate that a matter or truce we thought had been settled may be short-lived or is in danger of being subjected to unexpected changes. It may be cautioning us to wait for more information before concluding a matter.

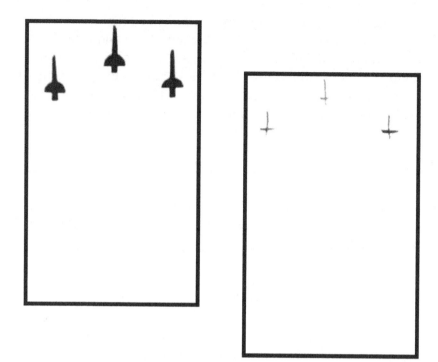

3 BINAH OF SWORDS

Essence: Indecision, worry or frustration traps us in an endlessly repeating pattern of negative thoughts. We are anxious and can obsess over fearful imaginings. We need to examine our assumptions and possible areas of self-deception.

The *Binah* (three) of Swords represents a time when our thinking is circular. Indecision turns to worry, to anger, to increased anxiety and obsessive thinking. Unable to break free of a fixed thought pattern we feel frustrated and trapped. This becomes yet another obsessive thought pattern.

Our rationalizations appear true. Self-deception or worries only dig our rut deeper. The problem requires we open ourselves to additional ways to understand reality. Sometimes thinking is not the only way to solve a problem. Here, the *Binah* reminds us that sometimes we can't think our way out of a situation or solve our problems. In that case, it may be wise to invite advice from a trusted friend or counselor, or to turn to books or other sources for help.

This is when we need to ask ourselves, "What other way can this problem be approached?

"Would even an arbitrary or spontaneous action help bring more options to light?"

"What are my feelings and emotions?"

"What intuitive sense or aid can I turn to, or trust?"

The *Binah* of Swords may be inviting us to go into our fears instead of denying them, so we can finally see through them to the truth of the situation.

REVERSED

When The *Binah* of Swords is reversed, the way out is harder. We may be in danger of drowning in self-hate or self-pity.

It may also indicate our focus is too outwardly directed and caught in the externals of the situation.

The *Binah* of Swords reversed can indicate there is an urgent need and benefit to be gained from seeking guidance from outside inspirational or emotional sources. It's strongly recommended we look to someone who can lead us to deeper awareness where we can explore our own inner wisdom, or introduce us to more profound sources of knowledge that can help us break out of fixed, obsessive or habitual thought patterns.

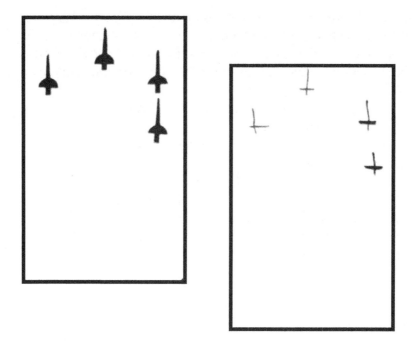

4 HESED OF SWORDS

Essence: Thinking is expanded until everything and anything can be rationalized. We have too much faith in our detached mental ability to solve all problems. Egotism of self-righteousness and self-deception is predominant.

   The *Hesed* (four) of Swords represents a time of extreme expanded mental energies. Our thinking is imbalanced. Everything can be rationalized. Ends are considered the justification for any means chosen. We may believe that power and the use of force is the only way for obtaining a desired outcome. We are being warned that our weapons are disproportionate to the task: an atom bomb dropped on an anthill; choosing a drug which is more dangerous than the disease it's meant to treat; a war where people no longer know why they are fighting yet still cannot stop. The *Hesed* of Swords may be an outgrowth of our frustration as a parent, spouse or friend. Having been tested to the limit, we find ourselves rationalizing abusive or bad behavior where we may say or do something we might regret.

Our actions in thrall to our imbalanced thinking may have a manic quality. It becomes important to slow down and think things through and reexamine our assumptions. We now must allow more time to evaluate our performance and look again at our motives.

With the *Hesed* of Swords we might ask, "What do I need in order to gain a better perspective of the situation? Isn't it time to take a breather?"

We need to stop for a moment, take a breath and see the absurdity of our position. It's time to let the light of humor in through our clouded thinking.

REVERSED

In The *Hesed* reversed we're being forcefully asked by some circumstance to pay attention to other aspects of life. Stop focusing on the solitary pursuit of some ambition or goal and focus within. When we look and listen to that inner guide, it can give us the answer and lead us to find a more effective direction toward which to focus our mental energy.

This reversal can be a warning we are in danger of physical disease. Mental and physical states are interconnected. It can especially refer to diseases such as fevers, infections, or any other malady that comes on suddenly and spreads rapidly throughout the body. Time to take preventive measures. Be aware the body is not just a servant of our great brain. Mental stress such as worry and anxiety may be better controlled, by focusing on the present moment rather than a not-yet-existent future.

This reversal reminds us that the body and immune system needs our attention, cleansing, nourishment, care, respect and love to thrive. Find ways to release or lower stress. And, even if we're having fun, conserve our energy. Take it easy!

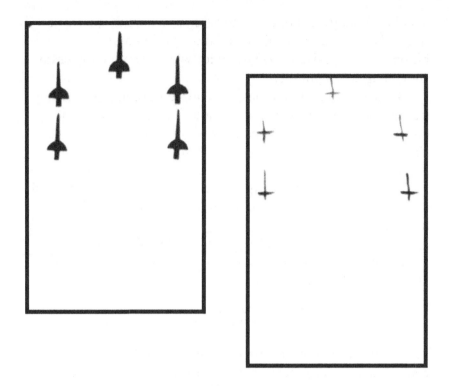

5 GEVURAH OF SWORDS

Essence: Narrowness of vision makes for dogmatic thinking. Perceiving our options to be limited or a lack of imagination may result in depression as we tell ourselves all is hopeless. We may become bitter and look to some despot or outside authority to think for us.

The *Gevurah* (five) of Swords refers to a contraction of mental energy. We are under the influence of closed- or narrow-mindedness, or are being shortsighted. Our vision is cramped. There is a danger of being enslaved by a dogmatic, habitual way of thinking or of perceiving reality.

The horizon of our possibilities seems low. Feelings of depression and hopelessness dominate our life. We may struggle to recapture the good old days. This can increase the likelihood of allowing someone who claims to be an authority to think for us. Narrowness of thinking and distrust in our ability to discern the truth or evaluate information may lead us to be overly dependent on the thinking of another, a cult or group who claims to have the *only* answer.

When subject to The *Gevurah* of Swords we may experience bitterness over wrongs done to us or be gnawed by feelings of remorse. We can't stop going over our past mistakes. It is important to gain a clearer perspective. Review the flaws in our thinking that keep us from trusting our own inner wisdom. Examine the present circumstances of our life; analyze our attitudes, fears, and emotions. The resulting self-knowledge can offer our best possibility for change.

Because of the nature of Swords and especially of the rocket-like formation of the Five of Swords, realize that under its influence this depression can be only a temporary state. It is within our control.

REVERSED

When this card is reversed, the mental entrapment may be more severe, taking the form of hatred or, especially, envy. Envy is probably the most contracted thought pattern, since it is not related to anything so much as our own projections. Envy is both selfish and malevolent. When we envy we suffer from the deluded thinking that if the subject of our envy is hurt we will feel better. If he breaks his leg somehow our leg will feel better, or if she loses her fortune we will feel richer. When we are consumed by envious thoughts we fail to appreciate our own unique gifts.

Envy can even make us literally sick at heart. When reversed, the *Gevurah* of Swords may refer to a danger of heart disease, which can also be a physical manifestation of hatred and envy.

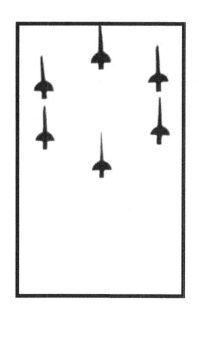

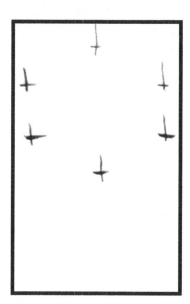

6 TIFERET OF SWORDS

Essence: Balanced thinking enables us to make good decisions. Seeing both sides of issues, we are fair, make better choices and can trust our own judgment and intellect.

The *Tiferet* (six) of Swords represents a triumph of intellect. Our mental energies function smoothly and well. Cutting through our illusions we are clear and insightful when making decisions or evaluating situations. Being self-aware helps us make choices that are beneficial to ourselves and others. We are able to act justly and treat ourselves and others with respect and fairness. The elements of justice and mercy are tempered and integrated. It is important to know we can trust our own judgment at this time. Able to perceive all sides of an issue, we see things in perspective and can trust our own advice will be the best, no matter what another so-called authority might say.

This is a perfect time for negotiating a lasting peace, settling a lawsuit or working out a compromise or clear agreement. Although all stands in perfect equilibrium, it is still important to attend to even insignificant details, if we really take advantage of the propitiousness of the time.

REVERSED

When reversed, this card implies we're getting what we deserve, which may or may not be what we want. This is a card of karma, but even karma is tempered with mercy in that there can be recognition that things done in the past may not be indicative of how we would handle them in the present. Thus, when this card appears reversed in a reading, it would be a good time to ask, "What pattern am I repeating, or about to repeat, which worked against me or didn't bring me a desired result?"

This is a time when we are capable of seeing our patterns and stopping or altering our habitual response.

It is important to remember that when we change, our karma can clear as well. since the function of karma is to teach, not to punish. As we evolve our karma evolves as well. We are encouraged to ask if there is something we need to learn from our present situation. This is a time we may look back over our life for the cause of any pain or unease, and heal it.

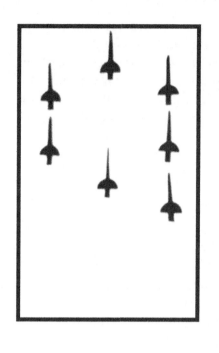
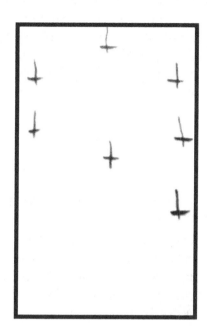

7 NETZACH OF SWORDS

Essence: Our constant search for answers has led us to the
realization of the subjective nature of reality. We're filled with
doubts and confusion. We question all authority. Seeing too
many possibilities and not wanting to narrow our options makes
decisions difficult.

The *Netzach* (seven) of Swords represents the experience of
the outsider or doubter. As a questioner, we have no belief in
authority, even our own. Here is a situation or problem we
cannot think our way out of. When we try to think things
through, we find ourselves entangled in options, opinions and
fruitless mental games and negotiations. At this time many
signals seem mixed or otherwise unclear. Misunderstandings
abound when we're not sure of what information means or

whom to trust. Each time we think we have found the solution, a new possibility negates it. We doubt ourselves, and others. Fearful of making a wrong decision we risk becoming hopelessly impotent. Through doing this we can miss the time for action altogether.

In the *Netzach* of Swords hesitation or confusion can be disastrous. This is not a time for halfway measures. We need to commit to a path of action and trust in the wisdom of the unconscious. It is essential if our endeavors are to be successful. Finally, if we remain frozen in indecision our choices may be taken over by another. This will not be to our advantage.

If we find ourselves circling yet never reaching the heart of a matter, we need to give thinking and analyzing a rest. Instead we should trust in our instinctive and spontaneous wisdom. When the house is on fire, there's no time to consider how to rescue the grand piano; we just grab the children and leave before the roof caves in. Sometimes it's appropriate for action to precede thought. This is the time!

REVERSED

When reversed, the *Netzach* of Swords indicates a situation where we should look before we leap and not let fear or a restless need for action make us unwilling to wait in the limbo of uncertainty. We must not now leap into action without sufficient thought or provocation. Our hatred of uncertainty and suspense may tempt us to push matters to a conclusion, any conclusion, even if it results in destruction and the manifestation of our fears.

For example, the reversal may indicate we're willing to accept a partnership, job proposal, offer of marriage, or legal settlement because we are fearful of not getting another one. Or we may agree to a medical procedure without waiting to get a second or even third opinion. If we do so we may find ourselves in an unfortunate situation that we could have avoided had we shown greater patience.

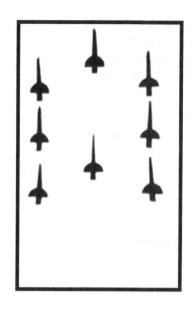
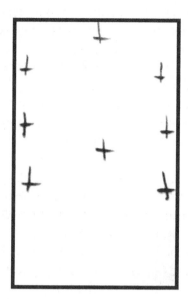

8 HOD OF SWORDS

Essence: Authority. The discomfort and fear embedded in doubt
has led us to seek an absolute authority. Or conversely, we may
ourselves claim to be one. Dogma is seductive. Fear of taking
responsibility subjects our freedom, choices and life to an
outside authority.

The *Hod* (eight) of Swords represents the opposite of the
Netzach. The pendulum has swung from the doubter to the
authoritarian. We are at risk of accepting the word of an
authority without questioning. All authorities, especially when
concerned with thought and understanding, are destructive and
possibly evil since they usurp our own experience and
perceptions.

Negative self-judgment is the base for the insecurity that
binds and restricts our ability for independent thought and

action. Insecurity-based fears cause us to retreat from our inner truth and look outside for the answers. We may be afraid of accepting responsibility for our choices or actions, and are therefore willing to submit control of our life to someone who claims to know better or even claims, "I know you better than you know yourself."

Our need for rightness may take the form of submitting our mental freedom and spontaneous creative consciousness to a restrictive inner authority and our own self-generated dogma. We may be stuck in the arrogant belief that our opinions and values are infallible. We can be as bound and enslaved by our narrow, rigid perception of a situation's possible choices, as we were in the *Netzach* of Swords when we were afraid of making a wrong choice or decision. It is essential to recognize the egotism of these fears and then to break free to make more creative choices.

REVERSED

When the *Hod* of Swords is reversed, we have accepted the authority of a negative parental voice. We have allowed this voice to undermine our self-confidence and our freedom of action. Words such as *You're not good enough, it's all your fault, how could anyone worthwhile ever love someone like you, you don't know anything*, bind us into a state of immobility. This causes us to fail to act in our own best interest. Intimidated and helpless, we are in danger of being victimized. We may even contribute to our own victimization through our inability to assert our rights.

If this is the case, it is important we develop a strong inner voice to counter the negative messages. A strong affirming inner voice can help us know, trust and assert our own truth.

Even if at first we don't believe the beneficent voice, with practice we can learn how to counter our negative, destructive messages. Statements like, "I trust myself to know what's best for me," or "It's okay if I'm not perfect, at least I'm working on myself," may help loosen the bonds of the situation.

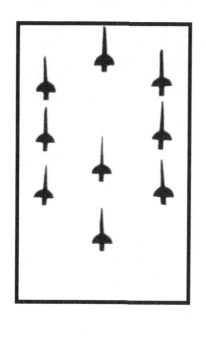
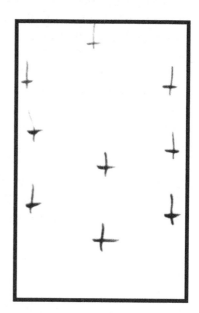

9 YESOD OF SWORDS

Essence: We want to give up. Our ambitions or desired relationships seem beyond reach. Our dreams are dust and we're tempted to feel hopeless or helpless. In nightmarish times, how we respond is our only choice. As we choose our response to this destruction, we become free.

The *Yesod* (nine) of Swords represents the clash between opposite energies. When all our efforts to create the life we want come to naught and our dreams are crushed, we are tempted to curse our life with statements such as: *It's all hopeless, nothing will ever work, I might as well abandon my dreams and live like a drone until death finally releases me.*

Our despairing thoughts spin in a maelstrom until we ask, "Do these statements empower, inspire or bring me closer to realizing my heart's desire?"

"Do my thoughts bring me joy, or make me happy?"

If our answer is "no," it's time to adjust our attitude. We can recognize that giving in to discouragement is a choice. No matter how difficult, our growth begins with being responsible for how we choose to respond to life's challenges. We may succumb to grief, negative projections and hopelessness. Conversely, we may continue on our path. Both are choices we make. Sometimes, when disaster strikes, our attitude toward it is the only thing we can choose.

We can continue in spite of all discouragements. Even if we go our entire life without attaining our original idea of success, we can look back and know we never gave up. We were courageous. We continued to strive. We were creative. Whatever the outer circumstances of our lives we took responsibility for our own happiness.

As the nightmare, the *Yesod* of Swords can subject us to the projections of our own fears or the fears of the collective mind, resulting in war, cruelty, destruction, guilt, and despair. We may, through confronting our internal demons, liberate our mind, even if we can't escape our physical circumstances. We are not passive recipients of our experiences, but create them each day.

REVERSED

When the *Yesod* of Swords is reversed the ability to choose our own way may be more difficult, or seemingly impossible. Our situation appears even more hopeless. Life may feel no longer worth living. Fear of facing the reality of our situation can make it even worse. The less personal responsibility we are willing to take, the more we inadvertently trap ourselves. We may feel sucked into a whirlpool of greater destruction and grief.

Finally, The *Yesod* reversed is a warning. It is important to pay attention to any misgivings concerning a situation. Our misgivings are probably well founded. Attention to intuition is essential. It can save us in a life-or-death situation.

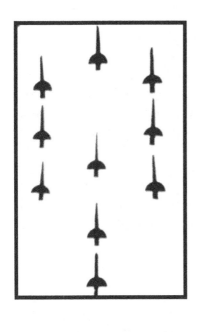
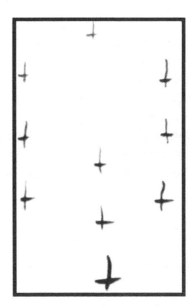

10 MALKHUT OF SWORDS

Essence: Thought's ability to solve our life problems has carried us as far as it can. Now our cool intellect merges with the warmth of the heart, becoming compassion, true wisdom and love.

The *Malkhut* (ten) of Swords is the end of thought. Thinking has reached its limit: the revelation that thought alone has not and cannot bring us the answers we seek. Those things which thinking has created have at best, solved only issues of communication, or pragmatic and technological problems. We learn that only when the lightning of thought merges with the deep ground of our heart can it become true intelligence, compassion and love. Thought now must come to rest before it can evolve to love. Love is ever changing: a vital, spontaneous, complete and responsible involvement with another.

At the height of our thinking ability we become self-directed, exercising conscious wariness that alerts us to our habitual thought processes. Detecting and naming the thoughts that chain us to our destructive emotions—paranoia, hatred, obsession, and envy—enables us now to detach. We are now willing to sacrifice our illusions and become mindful of our conditioning. Increasing consciousness can help us become free from enslavement. As we release those negative mental habits that lie at the root of all duality, sadness and fear, we begin to recognize our connection to ALL. We are awakening on the fertile ground of our immediate and perpetually changing truth.

REVERSED

When the *Malkhut* of Swords is reversed, our energy is not grounded. The Swords point down becoming a sharp rain descending to cut our imagined reality to ribbons. All we have clung to for security is shredded. The ground beneath our feet has shifted. We fear that mental anguish, death, ruin, sorrow, grief, fear or misfortune, are upon us. And they may be.

If this is the case, we can grow through this bad time by recognizing we may call upon resources other than thought to restructure our reality.

We need to remind ourselves that the one thing we can be certain of is change. Everything changes and so we gain the strength we need by focusing on our breath and on remaining present in the moment.

Or, we may choose to put off thinking about or dealing with a fear inspiring issue. Now we can safely allow ourselves to think about or deal with it at another time. We can remind ourselves that tomorrow is another day.

THE KING OF SWORDS

Essence: Reason is exalted, and the law. Ideals of fairness, equality, and of weighing differing points of view reign supreme. Also, an authoritative man ruled by intellect. Committed to reason and the life of the mind, he often denies or has little interest in the emotional or sensual aspects of life. He might be a scientist, mathematician, teacher, judge, diplomat, or counselor.

The King of Swords represents reason exalted. A man of authority, he may be a judge, or this card may signify the ascendency of reason and the law as such. He represents the ability to be rational, commanding, powerful, and objective. He can be a masterful problem solver or skilled diplomat. Concerned with and committed to ideas such as fairness, he is skilled at settling disputes. A wise and compassionate counselor, he is able to set aside his own emotions in order to view the subject as a whole. As well as law, research and scientific methods appeal to his temperament, making him a capable spy, detective, surgeon, scientist, successful in any occupation where gathering and synthesizing information or finding reasonable solutions is called for. He may also be something of an idealist.

More concerned with laws, contractual agreements, theories and proofs, the King of Swords tries to avoid being entangled by potentially chaotic, sensual or emotional elements. Intelligence here is experienced as an ability to collect and use information without letting our emotions get in the way. For the King of Swords, the life of the mind is his most profound commitment. He trusts absolutely in the scientific method and man's ability to rationally evaluate all information.

REVERSED

When reversed, it might indicate one so concerned with the letter of the law that he is lacking in areas of compassion or mercy. Convinced of his absolute ability to always act rationally, he can be self-deceiving, delusional, or even paranoid.

This card, when upside down, could describe a jealous and controlling personality who is capable of rationalizing anything. This person can be very dangerous, since he can inflict even the most monstrous tortures in the name of science, politics, religion or information gathering. Like the old patriarchal God or the ghost of Hamlet's father, the King of Swords reversed may demand vengeance, even to the destruction of his whole kingdom.

QUEEN OF SWORDS

Essence: An ambitious capable woman of powerful intellect. Her values reflect those of the patriarchy. Repressed and controlling of herself and others, she is observant, complex and manipulative. These qualities may make her an effective, sometimes ruthless leader.

The Queen of Swords is a woman who embodies the patriarchal values. She has powerful mental abilities and tremendous self-control. She can be graceful, charming, glamorous and extremely adept in social situations. Although no one really knows her, they may think they do. She can be a keen observer and interpreter of information. She is a complex personality, sly, devious and ambitious. The Queen of Swords is often interested in power and may function with great effectiveness and authority in the patriarchal realm. If necessary, she is capable of using her feminine charms to obtain her desires. Status and position have a strong attraction for her. With her clever quick wit and ability to articulate her thoughts, she can be absolutely ruthless when pursuing her goal.

When her tremendous energy is directed toward a humanitarian or beneficent pursuit, she can be an effective and dynamic force for social change, especially if her heart can be engaged.

It may be this archetype is a recluse or nun for she can be deeply committed to intellectual or religious study and ideals. Although the Queen of Swords may be a controlling and repressed person, on occasion she can be reachable when it engages her intellect or serves her purpose, or what she considers to be a higher purpose.

REVERSED

When reversed, the Queen of Swords may be a widow or a woman who has suffered great sorrow. She could be someone suffering with a chronic illness or physical disability.

This usually feminine archetype may when reversed be reflective of one who rationalizes the hopelessness of her position. By so doing she encloses her heart in suffering. This disease may stem from either a mental or physical origin.

The character of the Queen reversed can indicate a person who is consumed by bitterness or envy. She can have a cutting wit or she may be judgmental and sarcastic. She is one who can be devastatingly cruel without ever scratching the polished surface of politeness.

PRINCE OF SWORDS

Essence: This masculine archetype reflects the nature of one who, to understand information, must physically interact with it. Attuned to the physical world he is often mechanically gifted. He has keen intelligence and is able to cut to the heart of a matter.

This archetype, like all the archetypes herein, regardless of language used, might not only manifest as a male. It could refer to a female who also has these qualities. This archetype demands physical interaction to fully understand, process or ground any intellectual matter we are engaging with.

The Prince of Swords is a kinesthetic thinker. He might have a knightly self-image, seeing himself as a man of action rather than an intellectual. His intelligence usually lends itself to the sensate world. Being brave and physically daring, this archetype is one whose thoughts usually require physical expression. Since he often sees things in black and white, good guy/bad guy terms, he may be a law enforcement officer or soldier. He's the type of person who easily enters the active professions: fireman, police, navigator, explorer, pilot, bodybuilder, etc. Mechanically gifted, he is the guy who can fix or build anything. When his spatial abilities combine with physical skill and control he may be a dancer, athlete, builder or architect.

It's possible the Prince's keen intelligence and insight bestows an ability to cut to the heart of a matter. As well as a need for physical adventure, the exploration of the unknown, internal or emotional realms would satisfy both intellectual curiosity and the need for expansive self-expression. These traits could make for a physical therapist, explorer or even a dancer, actor or any type of performer.

REVERSED

When reversed, the Prince of Swords can be a card indicating a nasty, verbally abusive or violent and dangerous person.

He may be crude, a bully, or one who easily resorts to brute force as a means of attaining his desires. His thinking may be immature, self-centered, crafty, and lacking in empathy. Motivated by a desire for power or feelings of hatred, fear or envy, he can resort to criminal behavior, becoming at worst sadistic, dangerous especially to women, children and all others whose vulnerability makes them easy victims.

PRINCESS OF SWORDS

Essence: The Princess archetype describes a mentally quick, energetic and witty youthful person. It may be a warning against impatience and the danger of acting precipitously. It could mean the swift approach of an important message, possibly of a legal nature.

When the Princess of Swords refers to a person, it's someone who is mentally quick, energetic and witty. Often this archetype has a biting and insightful sense of humor. Using her wit like a rapier, she can cut others to ribbons or cut through to the truth of a matter. She can be iconoclastic, outrageous, daring and outspoken.

Like her brother, the Prince of Swords, she may also be a dancer or one who thinks with her body. She has a skillful, highly developed physical awareness.

Being enthusiastic and youthful, whatever her chronological age, her impatience may make her seem unsympathetic or insensitive when she is confronted with the troubles of others. Not being one to weep into her beer, she may be impatient with the bad luck of others or of her own bad luck, health problems and weaknesses.

The Princess of Swords may not refer to a person, but rather may indicate a messenger swiftly arriving with news. It can often indicate communication on a legal matter. Other cards in the reading determine whether the news it brings will be good or bad.

Sometimes the Princess of Swords, whether upright and reversed, can be interpreted as a warning against acting impulsively or without thinking. Too often our ill-considered words have a disastrous effect on our relationships. Many terrible accidents and even fatalities are also the result of careless or thoughtless action.

REVERSED

If in a reading this card refers to the Querent, it can be a warning that our own quick mouth can be our worst enemy.

As above, the Princess of Swords may be interpreted as a warning against acting precipitously. In this case the warning is even more urgent. Again, it's important to note that most terrible accidents and fatalities are often the result of an ill-considered, impatient or ungrounded action. Also, be aware there is a danger of attracting another's impulsivity to ourselves.

The Princess has appeared to warn us against indulging in behavior or weakness that, while appearing harmless and inviting, can be disastrous. Here the warning is to steer clear of anything which, while appearing charming, weak and small, might tempt us into thinking it will do us no harm. If we dally, if we ignore or underestimate it, it can tear our lives to ribbons.

When reversed, the person described by the Princess of Swords may be self-involved, controlling and lacking in compassion.

Princess of Swords reversed may also refer to a person with

some of the positive qualities listed above; however, she is cunning and prone to gossip as a way of attaining power. This might make her a dangerous and often hypocritical opponent.

Finally, this reversal may appear as a warning to look before you leap in regards to actions and relationships. Also, to not place trust in a person or message since motives may not be as harmless and transparent as they appear.

KETAR, ACE OF WHEELS

Essence: The material world where inspiration, emotion and thought unite, becoming the world of manifestation. We give concrete form to the dreams our energy creates. As the Wheel comes to earth, it may carry the arrival of a surprise, a gift or a vital message.

The image of the *Ketar* (Ace) of Wheels is of a wheel turning as it descends to earth. It looks like a wheel in my more formal deck. In my more informal, playful deck the wheel is a pizza. Both symbolize coming to earth, grounding our energy in order to create and nurture our development as it takes concrete form. Furthermore, the image of a pizza is used to express the delicious juiciness when all three elements unite in the material world. In Wheels the Primary Three Mothers, *Shin* (fire), *Mem* (Water) and *Aleph* (Air), represented in the Minor Arcana as the suits of Wands, Cups and Swords, join together, giving birth to the material world. In the *Ketar* of Wheels we give in to the impulse to manifest and enter the realm of the earth.

The fruits of our spiritual, emotional and mental efforts now come to ground. They bring with them the potential for prosperity, money, a new job, property, the first manifestation of any new-born creation, even a baby. What is wished for can now be granted. For better or worse, our prayers are answered. Labor and rest, growth and action, our potential to shape and be shaped is our capacity for building and giving concrete form to our dreams. We may make a name for ourselves, make our mark on the world, create a legacy.

If supported by the surrounding cards, the *Ketar* of Wheels may also indicate pennies from Heaven, an arrival, a happy surprise and the reception of a legacy, an unexpected gift.

REVERSED

When reversed, the *Ketar* of Wheels is a warning to be careful of what we ask for. It reminds us that things are not always what they appear to be. Some wishes, when granted, make the wisher wish they had never wished for it in the first place. Here is a reminder that every wish granted, everything we create, carries with it new responsibilities and commitments and demands more energy from us. As such, we need to prepare for the change, challenge and growth it brings. Here is a wake up call. If we are not grounded, this reversal, is reminding us we must now take the time to become grounded. If blessings come when we are not ready, the adjustment required may be more challenging, like having a child before we are ready and mature enough to take on the responsibility and challenge of our life focus changing from being about ourselves to the care for another.

2 HOKHMAH TWO OF WHEELS

Essence: Dissatisfaction with the status quo impels our creative efforts in pursuit of our goals. Desire for what we feel is missing in our material world, be it property, status, a child or connection to a person or persons.

The *Hokhmah.* (two) of Wheels represents a sense of lack, creating the desire for material fulfillment. We experience a need for money, status, a child, love, a home, or property—whatever it is in the material world we consider our self to be separated from.

Motivated by a sense of unfinished business or a feeling of lack, we seek fulfillment for some missing area of our lives. The *Hokhmah* may also be indicative of our yearning for a nonspecific object, something missing or something more, that now needs to be articulated so that we may discover and receive the satisfaction we crave.

Feeling complete yet unfulfilled without the object or success we desire can be a useful prod. It may stimulate us to realize that we actually have the potential for attaining our goals. We discover resources we never knew we had. We find we have the ability to delay immediate gratification, commit to a goal, and be willing to work toward the fulfillment of our ambitions.

REVERSED

The *Hokhmah* reversed can indicate that, because of the addictive nature of desire, we have become greedy. It may well be that even when our goal is reached or desired object obtained, it is merely traded for a new one.

It is possible that this reversal is a suggestion we need to cultivate our ability to be satisfied. We also are encouraged to examine more critically the nature of our desires.

When the *Hokhmah* is reversed our feelings of lack and need are almost overwhelming. We may have all our hopes and dreams pinned to something which even when attained will almost certainly not live up to our fantasy. Our yearning for an idealized object, goal or future can so overshadow what we already have as to render us blind to wealth we already possess.

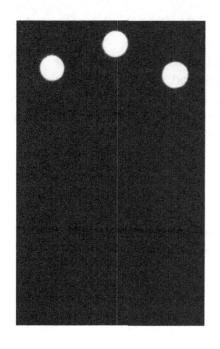

3 BINAH OF WHEELS

Essence: We have begun our mission. Although our way is clear and things seem to flow easily, there is much work to do. We need to plan and use our energy wisely. We realize we can't do it all alone, and find it's time to prioritize goals and enlist able helpers.

The *Binah* (three) of Wheels represents a time when wisdom and understanding are joined to the initiatory impulse. We now possess the right vehicle for obtaining the materialization of our dreams. We have the inspiration, grace, passion and skill to create our heart's desire.

The work has begun. We have the map and know how to use it. Our way is clear. Our plans for the house, job, marriage, or some other goal lie open on the desk; we're ready to create the foundation. It seems all our plans will come together almost effortlessly. While we enjoy this propitious beginning, we still must plan accordingly, prioritizing our time and energy in preparation for the labor ahead.

The *Binah* is a time to re-examine our goals and review our plans. When we accurately assess our strengths and weaknesses we know what skills require further development, what weakness need strengthening. In the light of this new information we can see with grater clarity. We may now decide to alter and possibly reorganize our plans. This may mean we realize we need to gather some new materials and or helpers that will be needed as our work progresses. Also re-examining our plans provides us with a chance to make whatever changes are necessary before it's too late, or too costly to turn back easily.

REVERSED

When The *Binah* is reversed it represents a warning against growing too comfortable or careless. It reminds us that now is the time we need to pay attention to even the smallest details of our process if we want the outcome to be successful.

Also, this reversal reminds us to plan for any unexpected or unanticipated problems that might arise. Since there can be unexpected changes in plans or in our situation it is important even at this early stage to plan for all eventualities.

4 HESED OF WHEELS

Essence: Expansive good fortune. Our way is open and
effortless. Everything we do comes out right and furthers our
ambitions. Nevertheless in fat times moderation is necessary so
as not to be caught short in the lean times which may follow.

The *Hesed* (four) of Wheels is like a gift from the universe.
There is great expansion in the material world. Money and good
fortune pour in. That for which we have been striving seems to
come with ease and grace. We seem to have the Midas-Touch. In
this time of great abundance we are suddenly able to attain the
object of our desires.

Enjoy the feeling of expansive abundance and freedom from
want, while still remembering to set a portion aside, in terms of
material wealth and physical and emotional energy, so that when

reversals come we have not depleted all our stores.

In spite of the appearance of total success, the *Hesed* reminds us that now, while we are living in abundance, we must use this prosperous time to be grateful, remembering that our good fortune is not a reward, is not only from our own doing, and to prepare for the lean times which may well follow. In anticipation of a reversal, it is essential to be moderate in our expenditures and to avoid wasting our time, energy or resources. If we are careful to gather and store nourishment before the famine comes, we will be protected and not taken unaware.

As part of our preparations we gather the able helpers we will need, assemble the colleagues and people who are trustworthy, capable and who hold the same values as we do. The work ahead will require collaboration, flexibility and possibly a group effort. It is also important to remain generous to our associates. If we are circumspect, we will make it through the lean time ahead and emerge from it with even greater prosperity.

REVERSED

If the *Hesed* is reversed, we are in danger of throwing ourselves away or wasting our resources. We need to consider whether we are allying ourselves with unworthy people or casting pearls before swine.

Conversely, we may be not listening to good advice because of the source from which it comes. It is important now to re-examine, and possibly value more highly, the advice we receive even if it comes from an unlikely source.

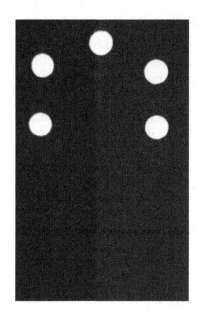 

5 GEVURAH OF WHEELS

Essence: We feel discouraged as all our efforts come to naught. The job or break never came. Time to review priorities, hit the reset button and start over. We need faith, trusting that with increased self-knowledge and perseverance, we'll find our way through this challenging time.

The *Gevurah* (five) of Wheels represents the arrival of lean times. Plans fall through. Good fortune we expected never materializes. It may be we lose or are at risk of losing a job. The stress and anxiety concerning our work, money or other resources now begins to have an adverse effect on our health and our intimate relationships.

We may be tempted to be stingy, fearful and overly self-protective. It is important to realize that this is no one's fault. It is beyond our control and merely a reflection of the times. Sometimes all we can do is trust and not allow the apparent hopelessness of the situation to discourage or keep us from believing in our deeper sense of purpose. We may need to have a good cry, a pity-party. Then it's time to review our priorities, re-examine our wants versus our needs, hit the reset button and change direction or start over.

All will turn around eventually as long as we persevere with our convictions. A generous attitude even in the midst of poverty helps. It may also help to re-examine our attitudes and beliefs to learn how they contribute to our misery.

REVERSED

When The *Gevurah* is reversed we may be even more fearful that our good fortune has flown away forever. This may in fact be the case. If so, we still have a choice as to our response, attitude and values. It may help to examine what might be learned from our present challenge. We may want to consider making adjustments to our life style and expectations. This can help fortify us in the face of any suffering.

This reversal can offer us an opportunity to develop new areas of creativity. We may discover inner resources that when cultivated can give us tools to transform ourselves, and our relationship to the situation. Then we can see it through new eyes.

It is important to remain responsible, fearless, open and able to respond to the demands of our times. Then positive changes begin to manifest. Even if literal wealth evades us our life can be richer with purpose and gratitude.

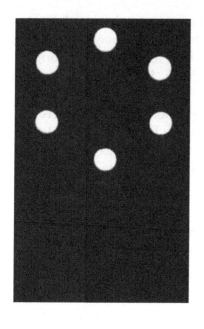
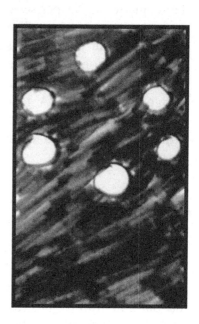

6 TIFERET OF WHEELS

Essence: As our material success becomes firmly established, we finish projects and tie up any loose ends. Expressive of gratitude and aware that no one ever succeeds alone, we are generous to others with our assistance and support. Prosperity must be shared.

The *Tiferet* (six) of Wheels represents a time when our material resources become firmly established. There is now enough for our own use, and we have the opportunity to share with others. Through generously sharing our good fortune we may find we gain even greater spiritual and emotional wealth as well as possibly increasing our prosperity.

Material success, coupled with generosity of heart, brings healing on all levels to ourselves and those with whom we are in contact. There is an opportunity to heal all our relationships with family, friends and work associates. In this context, material stability and success becomes a bridge and a link between people, enhancing our relationships. Freed from financial strife we have some breathing room. Now is the time to finish whatever we have left unfinished. As the spirit of heart-driven generosity can heal emotional wounds, this is the time to ask forgiveness for whatever hurt we have caused, and to forgive anyone who has intentionally or unintentionally harmed us. We are offered the opportunity to perfect and appreciate Goodness in the world we've created.

REVERSED

The *Tiferet* card reversed retains the essential meaning of its upright position. However, although we may have it all, our fear of loss and unnecessary hoarding of resources holds us back and keeps us from being generous.

Our fear of losing our material and/or emotional or spiritual resources may result in the loss we fear. Even if we retain our wealth, we risk losing the nurture of our gifts, talents, and relationships, all of which give meaning to the material. We then find ourselves impoverished no matter what our material state.

We need to overcome our self-doubts and develop greater trust in our resources and resourcefulness and in the Essential God-ness of life.

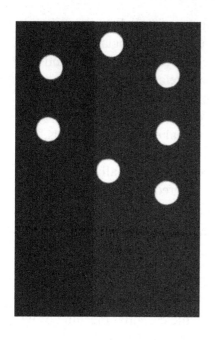

7 NETZACH OF WHEELS

Essence: Now we turn our attention inward. Although material satisfaction is still important, we focus more of our energy on living a meaningful life. Our allowing of others to support us relinquishes our need to be controlling. We can trust in others' abilities as well as our own.

The *Netzach* (seven) of Wheels represents a time when we are removed from the world of material fulfillment. Although the means for obtaining material satisfactions are available, we are no longer driven by other-directed ideas of success. We have an understanding of unnecessarily fearful visions of failure and of the pointlessness of striving after culturally defined illusions of success. Our values and attention are focused inward. We live beyond the realm of superficial concerns. We are no longer driven by shallow desires nor obsessed with outwardly directed symbols of security or status. The process of discovering security in the depths of the Greater Self becomes our main focus.

To set aside our false pride, let our vulnerability show and ask directly for what we need, we give others the benefit of being able to share their gifts and take care of us. As our ego releases our need to control others, we can appreciate others' abilities and skills. We realize that each has their own unique perspective and contribution that may enrich the whole.

REVERSED

When *Netzach* is reversed, we need to ask, "Am I trying to make others second guess me rather than asking directly for what I need?"

The *Netzach* upside-down can be an indication that we, or someone close, is being lazy and egocentric. We might explore whether our desire to share responsibility reflects a reluctance to complete an unpleasant task.

We may behave in a childish way to feed our need for power, trying to manipulate others to do for us as a means of control. Conversely, someone close to us may be trying to manipulate or control us in this same way.

There is a tendency toward parasitic behavior on our or someone else's part. We, or someone close to us, may be using ill health or physical weakness to avoid responsibility or to manipulate the other person.

This reversal can also represent a failure to take responsibility for spiritual, emotional or material relationships.

When we are honest with ourselves we not only benefit ourselves, we are also support our relationships and business interests.

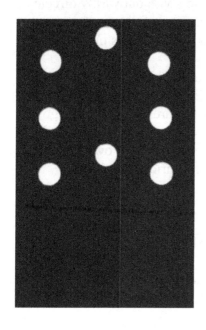
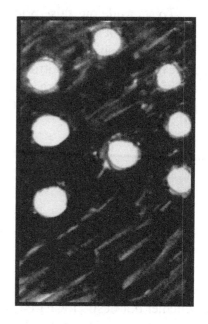

8 HOD OF WHEELS

Essence: We are excited about exploring new interests. As we develop a clear sense of our goals we can focus on expanding our education to that end. We gain the skills we need. We learn from our failures and mistakes as well as our successes.

The *Hod* (eight) of Wheels represents industry. It is a time of action. We are learning new skills, expanding our knowledge, responsibilities and contacts. This is a time to explore new interests, and for the development and refinement of skills.

We are willing to put forth the hard work and perseverance needed because we understand their importance as we pursue our goals. We also focus on building our skill at networking and the development of our community relationships.

Here, there is an interdependence of goals, skills and interpersonal relations. We recognize and are grateful for the support we receive and for all that has brought us to this moment.

REVERSED

When the *Hod* is reversed, it represents industry carried to excess: overbuilding, overproduction, hoarding and anxiety over resources and our abilities. Here is the workaholic so involved with money, power, or material satisfactions that they neglect all else. Our relationships suffer as a result, as might also our health. Family-, social- and love-life can deteriorate from neglect. It is important to slow down, relax and develop greater trust and better communication skills.

If we don't slow down and listen to other people's needs, interests, and ambitions as well as our own, we risk burning out our associates as well as ourselves.

If we can learn to focus on all aspects of our chosen work or project, we will realize what techniques and interpersonal skills we need to develop or refine. Then we can learn from our failures and mistakes as well as our successes.

It may be we are required to work at networking and developing our community relationships. We become willing to put forth the hard work, compassion and perseverance needed. We understand their importance as we pursue our goals.

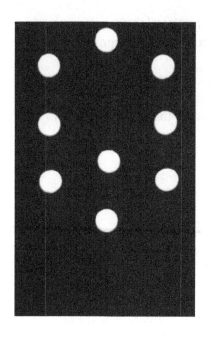
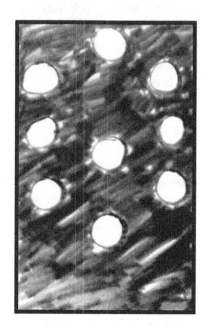

9 YESOD OF WHEELS

Essence: Now we need to find a new balance for our lives. We resolve divergent priorities and conflicting interests. Faced with our desire for creative self-expression and freedom, we are also committed to our responsibilities and desire for increased earnings.

The *Yesod* (nine) of Wheels represents the need for balance. We are in a state of internal conflict. We are conflicted about our living situation, personal relationships, or the demands of our work. Maybe we work at a job that is unsatisfactory in order to support a family. Perhaps our physical environment is incompatible with our needs or desires.

We now must move to reorganize our resources and resolve

the polarities in our life. This is a good time to re-examine our priorities and take a careful look at those aspects of our life that are not working. It is not necessarily any specific situation itself that is problematic; rather it is the balance and interaction between competing priorities that needs restructuring.

A clearer sense of organization, an adjustment in our living situation, or a re-evaluation of a relationship is needed. We are acutely sensitive to the impact our desired change might have on others, especially those who we love and for whom we feel protective.

This is a time for laying a foundation and advancing a new direction for our life.

REVERSED

The *Yesod* reversed could mean that sorting things out is more difficult. We may find our situation presents unexpected challenges. We struggle to understand our basic options, what is possible and what is not. We might even need a divorce or a new job. Either way, we need to find a better use of our resources.

It is most essential now to work on clear communication. Problems will be easier to resolve if we allow ourselves neither to be put on the defensive nor to be pushed to the offensive when attempting to confront difficulties. These issues may arise in family, work, school, or in any situation where we don't want to antagonize or hurt others.

Now is the time to work on our communication skills and commitments. We must learn how best to communicate that which troubles us rather than attempting to ignore it.

 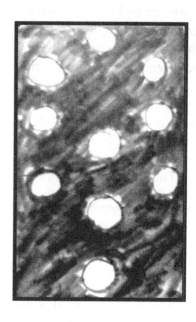

10 MALKHUT OF WHEELS

Essence: The *Malkhut* (ten) of Wheels is about gratitude. We feel thankful for all our blessings, all we have, all we've experienced and for our gift of life. We are grateful for however much or little we have and feel that it is enough. We are thankful for the people and relationships in our life, even the difficult ones. We love fully.

The *Malkhut* represents a balance and bringing together of all aspects of our life. Here we attain fulfillment through utilizing our spiritual, emotional, intellectual and material involvements. Our life is integrated.

The *Malkhut* of Wheels may also mean we've found a way to express our passion and have it support us. Our skills, emotions and sensitivities flow together. We've learned how to balance our relationship needs with our need for work and our experience of living a meaningful life.

Cycles of activity and rest are accepted and lived fully. We feel free, and can be fearless and joyful in all areas of our life. We are able to nurture the people we love and take care of our own needs at the same time. We are responsible and experience our connection to the Whole Holiness.

We accept change as essential to the ebb and flow of life's tides. We recognize that self-knowledge and learning involves the continual process of changing, integrating and deepening our awareness of life itself. Enlightenment is not a fixed state but rather the continual awakening of consciousness, of coming to know Truth.

REVERSED

When reversed, lingering fears and habits of thought hold us back from the realization of our wealth and a true acceptance of life. We may have it all yet somehow we're unable to recognize our good fortune.

When the *Malkhut* is reversed we are stuck in the perception that we are the object of our lives, not the subject. We are too passive. We don't own our life. Our good or bad fortune is seen as something that just happened, or was done to us without our participation. It is seen as something we have no responsibility for, not as something we have created or chosen.

We need to develop forgiveness. We need to forgive our selves and others for what we perceive as imperfections, weaknesses and mistakes. We even need to forgive the evil done to us. We realize we oppress ourselves with those whom we don't forgive. Until we finally learn to own our habits of repeating the same dysfunctional or abusive behaviors or relationships, and by owning them find the power to break them, we will be damned to repeat them.

We need to release our blame, resentment, anger, and hatred. Once we finally recognize that we are responsible for determining how we choose to perceive our life, we become free.

KING OF WHEELS

Essence: A *mensch* who is down to earth and capable. Whatever his profession, he will be skilled, trustworthy and dependable. A faithful and loyal friend, this archetype is often a family man, straightforward and kind with great ability for enjoyment of life.

The King of Wheels is a friend who is creative yet down to earth. He may be a good businessman or teacher. This card may indicate an older loyal male friend and good counselor, or possibly an uncle or stepfather. He is the epitome of what we mean when describing one who is grounded.

Any advice he offers in an area such as business can be extremely helpful and trustworthy. A responsible, caring person, he is appreciative and nurturing of growing things. He is helpful, straightforward, uncomplicated, openhearted and dependable. His energy is light, easy going, patient and slow to anger. He has a genuine enjoyment of life and an ability to balance work and play.

This card may also indicate a business associate who is pleasant and generous. The King of Wheels can even be a helpful stranger. He is often married, and whether or not he actually has a partner or children, by temperament he is probably a family man.

REVERSED

When reversed, this card may indicate an emotionally guarded man who, although affable, is basically uncommitted or unreachable. When angry, he can retreat into a stony silence and may be a rather unforgiving person.

At worst, this card reversed indicates an avaricious or miserly person of superficial values. He may be manipulative or hypocritical, more concerned with his own advantages in a situation than with anything else. He can be an opportunist, unwilling to make any effort that is not on his own behalf.

QUEEN OF WHEELS

Essence: A friendly and sympathetic woman. She is down to earth, honest with a clear, easy-going, nurturing energy. Generous, mature and capable, she helps foster the growth and development of those in her proximity. She may also be hard to get close to, or to know.

The Queen of Wheels is very much of this world. She is kind, responsible and good humored. She can be a good and trustworthy friend, empathetic and thoughtful of the feelings of others. She is capable, well grounded and possibly good in business, sales, teaching, or any occupation where a sympathetic temperament, combined with a discerning and intelligent mentality, is called for. She can be ambitious but is not usually petty or cutthroat. This card may represent an aunt or the mother of a friend, or possibly our own mother or mother-in-law. She may be hard to get close to or understand, as there is some mystery about her.

She is a nurturing person who helps foster our growth or development in some material way, either offering needed and useful practical advice and/or assistance, or through supplying physical nourishment or healing.

She can be a good gardener, either metaphorically or literally, enjoying and sharing the fruits of her creative nurturance.

REVERSED

This card reversed (like all reversed character cards) may indicate the archetype is describing one who is male instead of female.

Alternatively, in negative position, it may indicate we are being too insecure and dependent on outside influences. Lacking confidence, we rely too much on others for validation. We need to learn to trust our instincts and that our unique heart-felt offerings are enough.

IN HEALING
the damaged Holy's
bright fertile tears leak through each
imperfect shell's crack

This reverse placement may indicate we are dealing with someone who is overly concerned with appearances, one who is untrustworthy, greedy, opportunistic and overly fond of money and luxury.

She might have a tendency to become overly immersed in her work and have no time for deep relationships. This card may indicate that for all her friendliness she may be a hard person to get to know.

PRINCE OF WHEELS

Essence: A sensuous youth or one who is just young at heart. He or she may be a student: successful, free-spirited, athletic, and friendly. This person may be a good lover because of a sensuous nature and the pleasure they derive from giving pleasure to others.

When referring to a person, The Prince of Wheels is friendly and down to earth. When not referring to an individual known to the Querent, the card may indicate the arrival of a stranger, male or female, who can be of help to the Querent in some important and practical way. She can be a successful and powerful businesswoman or a teacher with a youthful outlook and the ability to inspire others with her ideas and, sometimes, her playful energy. This card might also refer to a student, or to one starting out on a journey or quest. He or she, is intelligent and sympathetic, a sensuous, pleasure-loving person whose ability to share their physical delight in life may make them a good lover.

The Prince of Wheels is open and honest and can be a loyal friend, loves animals and children, and can be a lot of fun to be with. He can be a helpful employee or co-worker. His advice is often both practical and relevant to the situation at hand.

He can be a creative and spontaneous person, yet his feet are always firmly planted in reality.

REVERSED

When reversed, this person can be hard to know or secretive. It may be a source of frustration when we attempt to get to any emotional depth. The reversed Prince can represent the type of person who appears to be open and warm with great potential for relationship, but who is actually somewhat remote and evasive when we get too close.

PRINCESS OF WHEELS

Essence: Unconditioned and unconditional love and joy, she is indicative of a fulfilling or transformative life changing message or communication--the dawn of a new day. She symbolizes the ability to act freely and snatch the brass ring on life's merry-go-round.

The Princess of Wheels may represent a message or letter, an important communication from afar. She may indicate a visitation--material, personal, or spiritual—from which we will receive a teaching or message that can transform our life. The Princess of Wheels represents unconditioned and unconditional love. The energy of this Princess archetype is androgynous and can be male or female. When she appears, she may bring a new chance and an invitation to view the world with a sense of wide-eyed expectation.

We now have the ability to act freely. We can grab the brass ring on the merry-go-round and ride for free. This childlike free spirit carries hope, joy and a miraculous gift or opportunity. The new day dawns as we see our potential fulfilled and witness the arrival of heaven on earth. As the last face card of the deck, the Princess is both a culmination of the past and a new beginning. Offered the opportunity of a clean slate, we can begin again, act spontaneously and create our own way.

When the Princess of Wheels refers to a person, she is the personification of innocence. She can be a child or infant, one with the wisdom of a child. She is magical, full of laughter and affection, like a lucky child whose dreams come true. She may also represent one who, like a beloved newborn, is a dream come true.

This final card of the deck symbolizes also a new beginning. We awaken to the world born anew. It is a time for gratitude and anticipation. Once again granted an opportunity to know what we are choosing, we are beckoned on to choose Life. We can give form to our dreams and create sacredness in our lives with the help of Holy Spirit, the Holy One.

REVERSED

The Princess of Wheels reversed may be indicative of a warning, omen, or karmic arrival. It also can represent a visitation, either material, personal or spiritual, from which we will receive a teaching or communication that can transform our life. However, in this case it could bring a more difficult lesson.

The Princess of Wheels reversed may serve as a warning that we are being too innocent, naive or foolish. It's time to grow up and take some responsibility.

A CLOSING THOUGHT

The Eternal manifests through all realms of the universe. As Kabbalah is a living, changing, evolving body of wisdom, a continuing exploration of the nature of God, so this book is an exploration and, hopefully, an inspiration and invitation to further and deeper understanding.

TORAH

White fire on Black fire
Flaming tongues weave worlds
Weave spaces
Weave into spaces
Between
Burning letters
Weave into words
Becoming worlds
Words
Climbing
Climbing
And the more words
The higher the flames leap
Until we burn
Until vision blurs
Until all that is not holy
All not whole
Is consumed
Holy

BIBLIOGRAPHY

The Holy Bible. King James Version. Published by the Syndics of the Cambridge University Press.

The Torah, a modern commentary. New York: Union of American Hebrew Congregations, 1981, (c. 1962).

Arguelles, Miriam and Jose. *The Feminine, Spacious as the Sky.* Boulder, Colorado: Shambala, 1977.

Ben Yehuda Eliezar, Ehud Ben Yehuda, and David Weinstein, editors. *The English-Hebrew, Hebrew-English Dictionary.* New York Washington Square Press, 1961.

Bettelheim, Bruno. *The Uses of Enchantment: The Meaning and Importance of Fairy Tales.* New York: Random House, 1967.

Bolen, Jean Shinoda. *Goddesses in Every Woman: A New Psychology Of Woman.* New York: Harper and Row, 1984.

Butler, Bill. *The Dictionary of the Tarot.* New York :Schocken Books, 1975.

Case, Paul Foster. *The Tarot.* Richmond, Virginia: Macoy Publishing, 194

Cavendish, Richard. *The Tarot.* New York : Crescent Books, 1975.

Cirlot, J.E. *A Dictionary of Symbols*, translated by Jack Sage. New York: Philosophical Library, 1962.

Cohn, Bill Bernard. *Stories and Fantasies from the Jewish Past.* The Jewish Publishing Society of America, 1951.

D'Olivet, Fabre. *The Hebraic Tongue Restored.* New York Weiser, 1921.

Samuel Epstein, Perle. *Kabbalah: The Way of the Jewish Mystic.* New York: Doubleday, 1978.

Fairbank, Alfred. *The Story of Handwriting, Origins and Development.* New York: Watson Guptill, 1970.

Fairfield, Gail. *Choice Centered Tarot*. North Hollywood, California Newcastle, 1985.

Franck, Adolphe. *The Religious Philosophy of the Hebrews*. New York: University Books, 1967.

Frank, Anne. *The Diary of a Young Girl*, translated by B. M. Mooyaart.
New York: Washington Square Press, 1952.

Frankl, Victor E. *Man's Search for Meaning, an Introduction to Logotherapy.* Boston: Beacon Press, 1962.

Galanopoulos, A.G. and Edward Bacon. *Atlantis, the Truth behind the Legend*. New York: Bobbs Merrill, 1969.

Ginsberg, Louis. *Legends of the Jews*. New York: Simon and Schuster, 1909.

Goen, John C. *Trance, Art and Creativity*. Buffalo, New York: Creative Education Foundation, 1975.

Goodman, Morris C. *Modern Numerology*. North Hollywood, California: Wilshire Book Company, 1945.

Graves, Robert. *The White Goddess*, amended and enlarged edition. New York: Farrar, Straus and Giroux, 1948.

Greer, Mary K. *Tarot for Yourselves, a Workbook for Personal Transformation,* North Hollywood, California: Newcastle Publishing, 1984.

Halevi, l'ev Ben Shimon. *Kabbalah: Tradition of Hidden Knowledge.*
London: Thames and Hudson, 1979.

Hoffman, Edward. *The Way of Splendor: Jewish Mystics and Modern Psychology.*

Holtz, Barry W., editor. *Back to the Sources: Reading the Classic Jewish Texts*. New York: Summit Books, 1984.

Jones, Mark Edmund. *The Sabian Symbols in Astrology*. Stanwood, Washington: Sabian Publishing Society, 1972.

Kaplean, Stuart. *Tarot Classic*. New York: Grosset and Dunlap,

1972.

Krishnamurti, J. *Dialogues and Talks*. Berkeley: Shambala Publishing, 1962.

Krishnamurti, J. *Education and the Significance of Life*. London Victo Gallanos, 1968.

Krishnamurti, J and D. Bohm. *The Ending of Time*. New York Harper and Row, 1985.

Maslow, Abraham H. *The Farther Reaches of Human Nature*. New York Viking Press, 1971.

May, Rollo. *Courage to Create*. New York: W. W. Norton, 1975.

Metzner, Ralph. *Maps of Consciousness*. New York: Macmillan Co., 1971.

Nichols, Sallie. *Jung and Tarot, an Archetypal Journey*. New York Samuel Weiser, 19.

Noble, Vicki. *Motherpeace: A Way to the Goddess through Myth, Art and Tarot*. San Francisco, California: Harper and Row, 1985.

Papus. *The Tarot of the Bohemians*. New York: Arcanum Books, 1958.

Ponce, Charles. *Kabbalah: An Introduction and Illumination for the World Today*. San Francisco, California: Straight Arrow Books, 1973.

Quigley, David. *The Romance Cycle: The Ladder of Consciousness, Sexual Energy Through Tarot Symbolism*. Self published.

Rockland, Mae Shafter. *The Hanukkah Book*. New York: Schocken Books,

Sachs, Hans. *The Creative Unconscious: Studies in the Psychoanalysis of Art*. Cambridge, Massachusetts: SEI Art Publication, 1951.

Saint Exupery, Antoine de. *The Little Prince*. New York: Harcourt, Brace, Jovanovich, 1943.

Schacter, Reb Zalman. *Fragments of a Future Scroll*. Mount

Airy, Pennsylvania: Binai Or Press, 1982.

Schoeck, Helmut. *Envy: A Theory of Social Behavior*. New York: Harcourt, Brace and World, 1966.

Scholem, Gershom G. *Major Trends in Jewish Mysticism*. New York Schocken Books, 1954.

Scholem, Gershom G. *On Kabbalah and Its Symbolism*. translated by Ralph Manheim. New York: Schocken Books, 1965.

Scholem, Gershom G. *Iohar: The Book of Splendor*. New York: Schocken Press, 1963.

Starhawk. *Dreaming the Dark*. New York: Beacon Press, 1982.

Starhawk. *The Spiral Dance*. New York: Harper and Row, 1979.

Stone, Merlin. *When God was a Woman*. New York: Harcourt, Brace, Jovanovicb, 1976.

Streit, Gary. *Romantic Love, Family Love: Two Talks on Love*. published, Streit, Gary, 1985.

Teubal, Savina J. *Sarah the Priestess: The First Matriarch of Genesis*. Athens, Ohio: Swallow Press, 1984.

Thomas, Dylan. *Collected Poems of Dylan Thomas*, the augmented edition. New York: New Directlons, 1957, (c. 1939).

Thorsten, Geraldine. *God Herself, the Feminine Roots of Astrology*. New York: Bantam Books, 1980.

Wang, Robert. *The Qabalistic Tarot*. York Beach, Maine: Samuel Weiser, 1983.

Waskow, Arthur. *Seasons of our Joy: A Handbook of Jewish Festivals*. New York: Bantam Books, Inc., 1982.

Weiner, Herbert. *Mystics: Kabbalah Today*. New York: Collier Books,

Wilber, Ken, editor. *The Holographic Paradigm: and Other Paradoxes Exploring the Leading Edge of Science*. Boston: Shambala Books, 1982.

Wilhelm, Richard and Cary F. Baines, translators. *The I Ching: or, Book of Changes*, Second edition. New York: Bollingen Foundation, 1964.

Made in the USA
Middletown, DE
28 July 2022

70105556R00146